# Understanding Your Borderline Personality Disorder

## A Workbook

**Chris Healy**

John Wiley & Sons, Ltd

**Other Wiley Editorial Offices**

John Wiley & Sons Inc., 111 River Street, Hoboken, NJ 07030, USA

Jossey-Bass, 989 Market Street, San Francisco, CA 94103-1741, USA

Wiley-VCH Verlag GmbH, Boschstr. 12, D-69469 Weinheim, Germany

John Wiley & Sons Australia Ltd, 42 McDougall Street, Milton, Queensland 4064, Australia

John Wiley & Sons (Asia) Pte Ltd, 2 Clementi Loop #02-01, Jin Xing Distripark, Singapore 129809

John Wiley & Sons Canada Ltd, 6045 Freemont Blvd, Mississauga, Ontario, L5R 4J3, Canada

Wiley also publishes its books in a variety of electronic formats. Some content that appears
in print may not be available in electronic books.

**Library of Congress Cataloging-in-Publication Data**

Healy, Chris.
    Understanding your borderline personality disorder : a workbook / Chris Healy.
        p. cm. – (Wiley series in psychoeducation)
    Includes bibliographical references and index.
    ISBN 978-0-470-98655-4 (pbk.)
    1. Borderline personality disorder–Popular works.  I. Title.
    RC569.5.B67H43 2008
    616.85′852 – dc22

                                       2008015506

**British Library Cataloguing in Publication Data**
A catalogue record for this book is available from the British Library

ISBN 978-0-470-98655-4 (pbk)

Typeset in 10/13 Scala by Laserwords Private Limited, Chennai, India

# Contents

**UNDERSTANDING YOUR ILLNESS**

Below are common questions that you, your family and others may ask when discussing your condition: Borderline Personality Disorder. These questions will provide the format for the sessions and hopefully provide you with information that enhances your understanding, so that you can lead a more positive life.

# About the Author

I first trained as a general nurse over 30 years ago and admit to feeling out of my depth at times regarding understanding those with mental health issues. I will also state that some of my ignorance and attitude was shaped by negative media reports. But since training as a staff nurse in psychiatry I have gained much insight and understanding of sufferers and their families.

I have worked for 12 years on a medium secure ward; most of the clients I nurse have committed crimes due to their illness. It is not common that those with mental health issues commit crimes but if their illness is left untreated and allowed to become more and more severe, sufferers who are acutely ill may unintentionally end up in prison.

# Preface

Sufferers approach mental health workers for information regarding their diagnosis and psychiatrists ask mental health workers to educate clients about their diagnosis. But how does a busy mental health worker achieve this?

There is much information on the Internet, in books and leaflets, but it takes time to bring together and organise this information. Most mental health workers will admit to struggling with collating up-to-date information and structuring sessions for their clients.

They may have printed off some information from the Internet, educated clients from their experience of nursing those with mental illness or read academic literature on the subject and summarised their findings. As a result, most clients receive different levels of education regarding the understanding of their illness.

This was the problem that I encountered during my nursing career, whereby I was in need of a format regarding basic information for my clients, and also a framework to provide structured sessions which would aid me in educating sufferers regarding their illness. So a few years ago I put together *Understanding Your Schizophrenia Illness: A Workbook* and this was published by Wiley-Blackwell in 2007. I have found that information in a workbook format allows sufferers to be more involved in learning about their illness and by writing down their thoughts and feelings their understanding is enhanced.

After I completed this first workbook I felt that there was a real need for sufferers of Borderline Personality to understand more about their illness as this is a much misunderstood condition.

Sufferers of Borderline Personality Disorder have difficulties in managing their emotions and behaviour which causes devastating results for those who have to try and live this condition and also those who care about them.

Over the past few years there has been increased awareness and research regarding this disorder which is helping to improve the treatment and understanding of Borderline Personality Disorder but at the same time it remains a controversial condition.

Regrettably, some health professionals have a negative concept regarding this diagnosis due to the difficulties of managing the care of sufferers with this disorder; also many health professionals would admit to having limited knowledge regarding this disorder due to it being a complex condition; but if sufferers of Borderline Personality Disorder can be motivated to change life long behaviours and learn how to tolerate uncomfortable feelings during treatment there is hope for a better quality of life for them and their loved ones.

Sufferers of Borderline Personality Disorder, their loved ones and health professionals need to believe that sufferers can make progress over time and lead happy peaceful lives; this workbook hopes to help towards achieving this.

The workbook is divided into six sessions dealing with various aspects of Borderline Personality Disorder. Each session begins with a questionnaire, to be completed by sufferers.

This is not a test but should be seen as a means by which the sufferer and their carers can share information. It will also allow sufferers to focus upon certain aspects of their disorder before each session. The sessions need to be completed at a slow pace, perhaps only a few pages a week, and it would take up to a few months to complete the workbook. It is important that sufferers work at their own pace to ensure that they thoroughly understand each session.

I would suggest that the workbook remains in the possession of a mental health professional until the workbook is completed. This is to prevent sufferers from working through issues alone in case they need some support. When completed, sufferers can keep the workbook and use it as a reference tool.

Please note that some of the self help coping strategies which are suggested throughout this workbook are not meant to be seen as a form of treatment but as a way of working through difficult emotions whilst the sufferer is engaged in some form of therapy, for example, talking treatment which is discussed in Session 4 and medication which is discussed in Session 5. Therapists may need to review some of the suggestions to determine whether they would be helpful to their particular client. This workbook cannot replace the valuable role a therapist has with regard to supporting and guiding sufferers along the road to recovery.

This workbook could also be helpful for health professionals as an assessment tool for their clients, and it could also be beneficial to detained sufferers as evidence that they have undertaken some work on understanding their illness when applying for a Mental Health Tribunal Review or Manager's Hearing.

It is our responsibility as health workers to provide education for our clients that enhances their lives and offers them some hope for the future. To this end, this workbook attempts to help sufferers to understand themselves better and find alternative ways of coping with their disorder much more effectively.

# Series Editor Preface

When sufferers are diagnosed with a mental illness, or have emotional and behavioural difficulties, it can be a worrying time for them; they will have many questions and will want to seek answers. Sufferers can approach mental health workers, where they can gain more insight into their difficulties and receive concise and up-to-date information.

Those who work with those who suffer from emotional difficulties are well aware that it takes a great deal of time to collate all the information and that, to help them, they need a structured format for working through mental health issues with their client.

The Psychoeducation Series aims to incorporate most mental illnesses, emotional and behavioural difficulties and will primarily be written by nurses who have vast experience and knowledge to share. The workbook's aim is to improve the knowledge of sufferers regarding a specific mental health diagnoses or other mental health issues through the use of structured interactive sessions. These sessions will also promote the nurse and client therapeutic relationship.

The series is not meant to be seen as a set of textbooks, but intended as a foundation of knowledge for sufferers to learn from professionals and, importantly, to work in conjunction with talking and pharmacological therapies.

# Acknowledgements

I would like to express my affection and thanks to Oz for his undying support and also to our family for their support and encouragement.

I would also like to express my thanks to Kishore Seewoonarain, Julia Asher, Lucette Long, Roger Culliford and Marilyn Long for their professional advice and support.

I would like also to mention my appreciation to Gillian and her team at Wiley-Blackwell for their supporting approach.

Finally, I would also like to thank my work colleagues for their support, but above all, it's important that I mention my clients who have given me much insight into their difficult world.

# Session 1

## ▶ Questionnaire

These questions are not meant to be seen as a test. They are only a means of sharing information and getting you to think about your condition before you start your session. If you are not sure just make a guess; there are no right or wrong answers.

1. What do you think personality means?

2. What do you think the general public's understanding is of Borderline Personality Disorder?

# Session 1

During this session we will be looking at the following commonly asked questions regarding Borderline Personality Disorder

1. What does personality mean?

2. What is a personality disorder?

3. What have people said about Borderline Personality Disorder?

4. What is it like to suffer from Borderline Personality Disorder?

# ▶ WHAT DOES PERSONALITY MEAN?

We often use the word personality but what does it really mean?

The term 'personality' comes from the Latin word 'theatrical mask' indicating that to understand ourselves we need to study the masks that we wear.

Our personality is 'who we are' and is something that makes us unique from other people, which includes our character, mannerism, qualities and our weaknesses. Our personality has an impact on how we behave, our moods and attitude which is reflected by how we get on with other people.

When we look in the mirror at ourselves, it seems intriguing that we are the person doing the looking but also the same person who is being looked at.

What do you see when you look in the mirror as the person doing the looking?

. . . . . . . . . . . . . . . . . . . . . . . . . . . . . . . . . . . . . . . . . . . . . . . . . . . . . . . . . . . . . . . . . . . . . . . . . . . . . . . . . . . . . . . . . . . . . . . . . . . . . . . . . . . . . . . . . . . . . . . . . . . . . . . . . . . . . . . . . . . . . . . . . . . . .

How do you feel when you look in the mirror as the person being looked at?

. . . . . . . . . . . . . . . . . . . . . . . . . . . . . . . . . . . . . . . . . . . . . . . . . . . . . . . . . . . . . . . . . . . . . . . . . . . . . . . . . . . . . . . . . . . . . . . . . . . . . . . . . . . . . . . . . . . . . . . . . . . . . . . . . . . . . . . . . . . . . . . . . . . . .

According to Murphy (1947) our sense of self or 'who we are' is made up of three main things.

Self image

Self esteem

Ideal self

We will be discussing these in more detail below.

## SELF IMAGE

Self image is how we describe ourselves and what sort of person we think we are for example.

There are two main categories for how we describe ourselves and they are:

■ social roles
■ personality traits

Social roles mean the position or part we play in society, for example, husband, sister, shop assistant or doctor.

Describe some of HM Elizabeth II's social roles:

...................................................................................................

...................................................................................................

Social roles can be confirmed by others, for example, HM Elizabeth II is a mother, wife, daughter, sister and the Queen of England.

Describe some of your social roles which say who you are:

...................................................................................................

...................................................................................................

...................................................................................................

Personality traits describe our character and our behaviour, which might be: friendly, assertive, dependable and creative.

Describe some of ex President of America Bill Clinton's personality traits:

...................................................................................................

...................................................................................................

Personality traits are different because they are more of a matter of opinion and judgement. For example, Bill Clinton might describe his personality trait as 'easy going', but some might describe Bill Clinton as 'competitive'.

Describe some of your personality traits which describe who you are:

...................................................................................................

...................................................................................................

...................................................................................................

As well as social roles and personality traits we often talk about our body image, that is how you feel about your physical appearance e.g. tall, thin, straight hair and attractive.

Describe your body image:

...................................................................................................

...................................................................................................

...................................................................................................

So, to recap, self image is a kind of mental picture that we have of ourselves e.g. who we are, what we look like, what we are good at and also what our limitations are.

How would you further describe your own self image, taking into account the above statement?

...................................................................................................

...................................................................................................

...................................................................................................

. . . . . . . . . . . . . . . . . . . . . . . . . . . . . . . . . . . . . . . . . . . . . . . . . . . . . . . . . . . . . . . . . . . . . . . .

. . . . . . . . . . . . . . . . . . . . . . . . . . . . . . . . . . . . . . . . . . . . . . . . . . . . . . . . . . . . . . . . . . . . . . . .

Much of our self image is based on the relationships we have with other people and also our life experiences.

This mental picture that we have of our self is linked to our self esteem. But what does self esteem mean?

## SELF ESTEEM

The word 'esteem' means to 'judge' (Collins, 2001) and is also a Latin word which means to 'estimate'.

So, self esteem means how you estimate yourself by judging and valuing yourself, it also has some bearing on whether you have a good opinion of yourself or not.

What would you say best describes the opinion you have of yourself?

. . . . . . . . . . . . . . . . . . . . . . . . . . . . . . . . . . . . . . . . . . . . . . . . . . . . . . . . . . . . . . . . . . . . . . . .

. . . . . . . . . . . . . . . . . . . . . . . . . . . . . . . . . . . . . . . . . . . . . . . . . . . . . . . . . . . . . . . . . . . . . . . .

. . . . . . . . . . . . . . . . . . . . . . . . . . . . . . . . . . . . . . . . . . . . . . . . . . . . . . . . . . . . . . . . . . . . . . . .

Coopersmith (1967) defined self esteem as the degree to how much we like, accept or approve ourselves.

- Do I like myself?
- Do I deserve happiness?
- Am I an OK sort of person?
- Do I deserve someone to love me?
- Am I a good person?

Those with a low self esteem would find it difficult to answer yes to these questions, mainly because they feel no one will like them and that they can't do anything well.

On the other hand, people with a healthy self esteem are able to feel good about themselves:

- I like myself.
- I am a good person.
- I deserve happiness.
- I deserve to be loved.

Would you say you had a healthy or a low self esteem?

. . . . . . . . . . . . . . . . . . . . . . . . . . . . . . . . . . . . . . . . . . . . . . . . . . . . . . . . . . . . . . . . . . . . . . . .

Which statements above have you used to rate yourself?

. . . . . . . . . . . . . . . . . . . . . . . . . . . . . . . . . . . . . . . . . . . . . . . . . . . . . . . . . . . . . . . . . . . . . . . .

..................................................................................

..................................................................................

..................................................................................

..................................................................................

So how does our self esteem develop?

Self esteem is mostly developed by outside influences, that is, what someone told us about ourselves whether it be good or bad.

- How we were treated by our parents e.g. praise or criticisms.
- How we were treated by our teachers e.g. praise or criticisms.
- How we are treated by peers e.g. bullying or being accepted by peers.
- Media images of, for example, skinny women and muscular men.
- Racial and prejudices issues.

Do you think that any of the above had an influence on the development of your self esteem?

..................................................................................

..................................................................................

..................................................................................

..................................................................................

So, self esteem is all about how much we feel valued, loved and accepted by others and how much we value, love and accept ourselves.

## IDEAL SELF

Our ideal self is the personality we would like to be and consists of our dreams, ambitions and a belief in ourselves.

What sort of person would you like to be?

..................................................................................

..................................................................................

..................................................................................

..................................................................................

..................................................................................

The larger the gap between our self image (that is, who we think we are) and our ideal self (that is, who we want to be), the lower our self esteem will be. How we feel about ourselves can influence the way we live our lives, and people who feel they are likable will have better relationships than those who don't like themselves.

The development of our personality is also influenced by a number of other things which include:

> **Genetics** – inherited from our relatives (Plomin *et al.*, 2001)

Do you have similar personality traits e.g. temperament and behaviour to some members of your family?

. . . . . . . . . . . . . . . . . . . . . . . . . . . . . . . . . . . . . . . . . . . . . . . . . . . . . . . . . . . . . . . . . . . . .

. . . . . . . . . . . . . . . . . . . . . . . . . . . . . . . . . . . . . . . . . . . . . . . . . . . . . . . . . . . . . . . . . . . . .

. . . . . . . . . . . . . . . . . . . . . . . . . . . . . . . . . . . . . . . . . . . . . . . . . . . . . . . . . . . . . . . . . . . . .

> **Birth order** – whether we are the youngest, middle, eldest or only child (Sulloway, 1997)

What position are you in birth order to your brothers or sisters and do you see a resemblance between yourself and other people you know in the same birth order?

. . . . . . . . . . . . . . . . . . . . . . . . . . . . . . . . . . . . . . . . . . . . . . . . . . . . . . . . . . . . . . . . . . . . .

. . . . . . . . . . . . . . . . . . . . . . . . . . . . . . . . . . . . . . . . . . . . . . . . . . . . . . . . . . . . . . . . . . . . .

. . . . . . . . . . . . . . . . . . . . . . . . . . . . . . . . . . . . . . . . . . . . . . . . . . . . . . . . . . . . . . . . . . . . .

> **Gender** – how we are treated as a male and female (Beal, 1993)

Do you think your gender is treated differently to other genders?

. . . . . . . . . . . . . . . . . . . . . . . . . . . . . . . . . . . . . . . . . . . . . . . . . . . . . . . . . . . . . . . . . . . . .

. . . . . . . . . . . . . . . . . . . . . . . . . . . . . . . . . . . . . . . . . . . . . . . . . . . . . . . . . . . . . . . . . . . . .

. . . . . . . . . . . . . . . . . . . . . . . . . . . . . . . . . . . . . . . . . . . . . . . . . . . . . . . . . . . . . . . . . . . . .

> **Environment** – shaped by events of our early childhood or adolescence and if the experiences have been awful it can alter a person's inner self (Harris, 2006)

Do you think your personality has been influenced by your environment?

. . . . . . . . . . . . . . . . . . . . . . . . . . . . . . . . . . . . . . . . . . . . . . . . . . . . . . . . . . . . . . . . . . . . .

. . . . . . . . . . . . . . . . . . . . . . . . . . . . . . . . . . . . . . . . . . . . . . . . . . . . . . . . . . . . . . . . . . . . .

. . . . . . . . . . . . . . . . . . . . . . . . . . . . . . . . . . . . . . . . . . . . . . . . . . . . . . . . . . . . . . . . . . . . .

Those who suffer from Borderline Personality Disorder usually have difficulties with relationships both with themselves and others and also develop a low self esteem, but it is hoped that through this workbook you will understand your own personality and make some sense of how you see yourself, others and your world.

## ► WHAT IS A PERSONALITY DISORDER?

Personality Disorder was first defined 200 years ago 1801 by a French psychiatrist Philippe Pinel, who came up with the term 'manic sans delire' describing a condition whereby there 'was no change in intellectual functioning but there was an evident disorder of mood functioning, including impulsive behaviour'.

The World Health Organisation (ICD-10) and the American Psychiatric Association (DSM-IV) have different classifications regarding mental disorders and over the years have not been able to agree on the definition of a personality disorder.

But the current classifications on the disorder are:

> **'a pattern of inner experience and behaviour that deviates from the expectation of the individuals' culture, which leads to distress and impairment'.** (DSM- IV, 1994)
>
> **'a severe disturbance in behavioural tendencies of the individual and nearly always associated with considerable personal and social disruption'.** (ICD-10, 1992)

What have you understood from the above classifications?

.................................................................................................

.................................................................................................

.................................................................................................

If you have not understood the above classification speak to your mental health worker as it can be confusing trying to understand your condition.

ICD-10 describes Borderline Personality Disorder as an 'emotionally unstable personality disorder' but both ICD 10 and DSM-IV are currently revising their classifications.

The first draft for ICD-11 is expected in 2008 and should be implemented in 2013 with DSM-V in approximately 2011. It is being considered whether to replace the DSM-IV with an alternative diagnostic system based on the five-factor model.

This five-factor model is known as OCEAN which stands for Openness, Conscientiousness, Extraversion, Agreeableness and Neuroticism (Widiger *et al.*, 2002).

As already mentioned our personality is a complex mixture of unique traits which include characteristics like generosity and shyness and these influence our thoughts and feelings.

Our traits are ways for us to observe, react and think about the world we live in and they also give us a sense of who we are.

A personality disorder is diagnosed when several areas of someone's personality are causing them problems in everyday life which may cause themselves or others to suffer. This might be problems regarding their:

- self image
- communication with others
- way of seeing themselves
- control of their impulses.

Has the way in which you think, feel and behave caused you any difficulties?

. . . . . . . . . . . . . . . . . . . . . . . . . . . . . . . . . . . . . . . . . . . . . . . . . . . . . . . . . . . . . . . . . . . . . . . . . . . . . . . . . . . . . . . . . . . . . . .

. . . . . . . . . . . . . . . . . . . . . . . . . . . . . . . . . . . . . . . . . . . . . . . . . . . . . . . . . . . . . . . . . . . . . . . . . . . . . . . . . . . . . . . . . . . . . . .

. . . . . . . . . . . . . . . . . . . . . . . . . . . . . . . . . . . . . . . . . . . . . . . . . . . . . . . . . . . . . . . . . . . . . . . . . . . . . . . . . . . . . . . . . . . . . . .

Personality disorder is when a person has difficulties coping with life and where their behaviour persistently causes distress to themselves or others.

There are ten different types of personality disorder (DSM-1V) and they are:

| |
|---|
| Paranoid Personality Disorder |
| Schizoid Personality Disorder |
| Schizotypal Personality Disorder |
| Histrionic Personality Disorder |
| Narcissistic Personality Disorder |
| Avoidant (or anxious) Personality Disorder |
| Antisocial Personality Disorder |
| Dependent Personality Disorder |
| Obsessive-compulsive Personality Disorder |
| Borderline Personality Disorder |

There is no laboratory test to find out whether someone has a personality disorder; a diagnosis is made on the basis of the sufferer's history details and some personality tests which include answering true or false statements about your thoughts, feelings and behaviour. Another test is the 'inkblot', that is, interpreting shapes which examine your inner feelings, motives and perception of the world.

Have you undergone any personality test?

.............................................................................................

.............................................................................................

As mentioned above there are ten different personality disorders (DSM-IV) but for this workbook we will only focus on Borderline Personality Disorder.

In Britain the diagnosis of personality disorder ranges from 2 per cent to 13 per cent in the general population (*BJM*, 1997) Usually those with Borderline Personality Disorder are also diagnosed with other conditions, for example, depression, phobias, post traumatic stress, obsessive compulsive disorder, generalised anxiety disorder. Speak to your nurse or doctor about these conditions.

So to recap, a personality disorder is a condition which affects the way you think, feel and behave and due to this, it causes you much difficulty in trying to cope or understand your emotions and behaviour, which can be upsetting and disturbing for yourself and other people.

Would you agree with the above statement?

.............................................................................................

Why?

.............................................................................................

.............................................................................................

.............................................................................................

.............................................................................................

## ▶ WHAT HAVE PEOPLE SAID ABOUT BORDERLINE PERSONALITY DISORDER?

Some of those suffering from Borderline Personality Disorder have been portrayed in a discourteous and derogative way.

The most common belittling terms used are:

- attention seeking
- untreatable
- bad or mad
- needy
- don't deserve treatment
- inadequate
- difficult
- selfish
- weak
- troublemaker.

Have you come across any of the above terms and if so how did it make you feel?

........................................................................................

........................................................................................

........................................................................................

........................................................................................

> If you have been diagnosed as suffering from Borderline Personality Disorder and are familiar with these descriptions then let it be known that none of the above is true. You undoubtedly deserve care and attention and with successful treatment you indeed can recover.

## ▶ WHAT IS IT LIKE TO SUFFER FROM BORDERLINE PERSONALITY DISORDER?

It is really hard to describe what it is like to suffer from Borderline Personality Disorder, but non sufferers can only guess what it must be like. Do you go through cycles of feeling miserable, angry and calm on a regular basis and can you answer yes to most of the following:

Do you have periods of good and bad moods?

........................................................................................

........................................................................................

........................................................................................

Do you have a great fear of being rejected?

........................................................................................

........................................................................................

........................................................................................

Are you terrified of being alone?

........................................................................................

........................................................................................

........................................................................................

Do you constantly feel bored and have a lack of purpose in your life?

........................................................................................

........................................................................................

........................................................................................

Do you experience feeling of emptiness?

........................................................................................

........................................................................................

........................................................................................

Those who do not suffer from Borderline Personality Disorder find it very hard to understand the experiences of those who do. It can be a worrying experience, especially for families and friends, to see their loved ones suffering and not know how to help them.

## ▶ End-of-session Questionnaire

What three important things have you learnt and will take away with you from Session 1 (you may need to browse through the session again to jog your memory).

1 . . . . . . . . . . . . . . . . . . . . . . . . . . . . . . . . . . . . . . . . . . . . . . . . . . . . . . . . . . . . . . . . . . . . . . . . . . . . . . . . . .
. . . . . . . . . . . . . . . . . . . . . . . . . . . . . . . . . . . . . . . . . . . . . . . . . . . . . . . . . . . . . . . . . . . . . . . . . . . . . . . . . .
. . . . . . . . . . . . . . . . . . . . . . . . . . . . . . . . . . . . . . . . . . . . . . . . . . . . . . . . . . . . . . . . . . . . . . . . . . . . . . . . . .
. . . . . . . . . . . . . . . . . . . . . . . . . . . . . . . . . . . . . . . . . . . . . . . . . . . . . . . . . . . . . . . . . . . . . . . . . . . . . . . . . .
. . . . . . . . . . . . . . . . . . . . . . . . . . . . . . . . . . . . . . . . . . . . . . . . . . . . . . . . . . . . . . . . . . . . . . . . . . . . . . . . . .
. . . . . . . . . . . . . . . . . . . . . . . . . . . . . . . . . . . . . . . . . . . . . . . . . . . . . . . . . . . . . . . . . . . . . . . . . . . . . . . . . .
. . . . . . . . . . . . . . . . . . . . . . . . . . . . . . . . . . . . . . . . . . . . . . . . . . . . . . . . . . . . . . . . . . . . . . . . . . . . . . . . . .
. . . . . . . . . . . . . . . . . . . . . . . . . . . . . . . . . . . . . . . . . . . . . . . . . . . . . . . . . . . . . . . . . . . . . . . . . . . . . . . . . .
. . . . . . . . . . . . . . . . . . . . . . . . . . . . . . . . . . . . . . . . . . . . . . . . . . . . . . . . . . . . . . . . . . . . . . . . . . . . . . . . . .

2 . . . . . . . . . . . . . . . . . . . . . . . . . . . . . . . . . . . . . . . . . . . . . . . . . . . . . . . . . . . . . . . . . . . . . . . . . . . . . . . . . .
. . . . . . . . . . . . . . . . . . . . . . . . . . . . . . . . . . . . . . . . . . . . . . . . . . . . . . . . . . . . . . . . . . . . . . . . . . . . . . . . . .
. . . . . . . . . . . . . . . . . . . . . . . . . . . . . . . . . . . . . . . . . . . . . . . . . . . . . . . . . . . . . . . . . . . . . . . . . . . . . . . . . .
. . . . . . . . . . . . . . . . . . . . . . . . . . . . . . . . . . . . . . . . . . . . . . . . . . . . . . . . . . . . . . . . . . . . . . . . . . . . . . . . . .
. . . . . . . . . . . . . . . . . . . . . . . . . . . . . . . . . . . . . . . . . . . . . . . . . . . . . . . . . . . . . . . . . . . . . . . . . . . . . . . . . .
. . . . . . . . . . . . . . . . . . . . . . . . . . . . . . . . . . . . . . . . . . . . . . . . . . . . . . . . . . . . . . . . . . . . . . . . . . . . . . . . . .
. . . . . . . . . . . . . . . . . . . . . . . . . . . . . . . . . . . . . . . . . . . . . . . . . . . . . . . . . . . . . . . . . . . . . . . . . . . . . . . . . .
. . . . . . . . . . . . . . . . . . . . . . . . . . . . . . . . . . . . . . . . . . . . . . . . . . . . . . . . . . . . . . . . . . . . . . . . . . . . . . . . . .

3 . . . . . . . . . . . . . . . . . . . . . . . . . . . . . . . . . . . . . . . . . . . . . . . . . . . . . . . . . . . . . . . . . . . . . . . . . . . . . . . . . .
. . . . . . . . . . . . . . . . . . . . . . . . . . . . . . . . . . . . . . . . . . . . . . . . . . . . . . . . . . . . . . . . . . . . . . . . . . . . . . . . . .
. . . . . . . . . . . . . . . . . . . . . . . . . . . . . . . . . . . . . . . . . . . . . . . . . . . . . . . . . . . . . . . . . . . . . . . . . . . . . . . . . .
. . . . . . . . . . . . . . . . . . . . . . . . . . . . . . . . . . . . . . . . . . . . . . . . . . . . . . . . . . . . . . . . . . . . . . . . . . . . . . . . . .
. . . . . . . . . . . . . . . . . . . . . . . . . . . . . . . . . . . . . . . . . . . . . . . . . . . . . . . . . . . . . . . . . . . . . . . . . . . . . . . . . .
. . . . . . . . . . . . . . . . . . . . . . . . . . . . . . . . . . . . . . . . . . . . . . . . . . . . . . . . . . . . . . . . . . . . . . . . . . . . . . . . . .
. . . . . . . . . . . . . . . . . . . . . . . . . . . . . . . . . . . . . . . . . . . . . . . . . . . . . . . . . . . . . . . . . . . . . . . . . . . . . . . . . .
. . . . . . . . . . . . . . . . . . . . . . . . . . . . . . . . . . . . . . . . . . . . . . . . . . . . . . . . . . . . . . . . . . . . . . . . . . . . . . . . . .

# Session 2

## ▶ Questionnaire

These questions are not meant to be seen as a test. They are only a means of sharing information and getting you to think about your condition before you start your session. If you are not sure make a guess; there are no right or wrong answers.

1. Do you know what people have said causes Borderline Personality Disorder?

2. Do you know of any famous person who has been said to suffer from personality disorder?

# Session 2

During this session we will be looking at the most commonly asked questions about the causes of Borderline Personality Disorder.

1. Can you inherit Borderline Personality Disorder?

2. Is it something to do with the brain?

3. Does the environment in which you grew up cause you to develop Borderline Personality Disorder?

4. What famous people suffer from Borderline Personality Disorder?

# Session 2

At present no one can find a single reason for what causes Borderline Personality Disorder, but there is likely to be a number of triggers involved and really there is no knowing who will develop the condition.

Some of the theories that have been put forward have been:

**Genetic theory**, that is, you can inherit it from your family.

**Brain abnormality theory**, that is, your brain is different in some way.

**Environment theory**, that is, something to do with your personal history.

## ▶ CAN YOU INHERIT BORDERLINE PERSONALITY DISORDER?

There have been some studies on twins and families which suggest that personality disorders may be inherited (Torgersen *et al.*, 2000).

Does a member of your family also suffer from Borderline Personality Disorder?

. . . . . . . . . . . . . . . . . . . . . . . . . . . . . . . . . . . . . . . . . . . . . . . . . . . . . . . . . . . . . . . . . . . . . . . . . . . . .

. . . . . . . . . . . . . . . . . . . . . . . . . . . . . . . . . . . . . . . . . . . . . . . . . . . . . . . . . . . . . . . . . . . . . . . . . . . . .

It has been said that you are at risk of developing the condition if a close member of your family also suffers from Borderline Personality Disorder. There is no statistic data in the UK, but the risk of developing Borderline Personality Disorder due to hereditary factors are much lower than environmental factors which will be discussed later.

## ▶ IS IT SOMETHING TO DO WITH THE BRAIN?

What do you know about the brain?

. . . . . . . . . . . . . . . . . . . . . . . . . . . . . . . . . . . . . . . . . . . . . . . . . . . . . . . . . . . . . . . . . . . . . . . . . . . . .

. . . . . . . . . . . . . . . . . . . . . . . . . . . . . . . . . . . . . . . . . . . . . . . . . . . . . . . . . . . . . . . . . . . . . . . . . . . . .

. . . . . . . . . . . . . . . . . . . . . . . . . . . . . . . . . . . . . . . . . . . . . . . . . . . . . . . . . . . . . . . . . . . . . . . . . . . . .

. . . . . . . . . . . . . . . . . . . . . . . . . . . . . . . . . . . . . . . . . . . . . . . . . . . . . . . . . . . . . . . . . . . . . . . . . . . . .

. . . . . . . . . . . . . . . . . . . . . . . . . . . . . . . . . . . . . . . . . . . . . . . . . . . . . . . . . . . . . . . . . . . . . . . . . . . . .

. . . . . . . . . . . . . . . . . . . . . . . . . . . . . . . . . . . . . . . . . . . . . . . . . . . . . . . . . . . . . . . . . . . . . . . . . . . . .

Your brain's tasks are:

- Controlling your body temperature, blood pressure, heart rate and breathing.
- Taking in information from your senses (eyes, nose, ears, and so on) about what is going on around you.
- Responsibility for your physical movements like walking, talking, sitting or standing.
- Allowing you to think, dream and experience emotions.

The brain and the rest of the nervous system are made up of many different cells, but the main nerve cell is called a neurone.

How many neurones do you think we might need to do all this work?

. . . . . . . . . . . . . . . . . . . . . . . . . . . . . . . . . . . . . . . . . . . . . . . . . . . . . . . . . . . . . . . . . . . . . . . . . . . . . .

We have billions of these neurones, and these neurones have the ability to gather and transmit messages from the brain to the rest of the body much like the circuit in a computer.

Scientists have learnt a lot about these nerve cells or neurones by studying the 'synapse'. A synapse is a small gap which separates one nerve cell from another and is the place where information gets passed from one nerve cell to the next nerve cell with the help of special chemicals called 'neurotransmitters'.

It is here where it is thought that the brain may play a role in Borderline Personality Disorder. It is said that sufferers have an imbalance, for example, 'too low' of several of these chemicals.

The main chemical is called Serotonin and the medications that help to control the symptoms of Borderline Personality Disorder seem to help increase the levels of these chemicals.

This neurotransmitter Serotonin is responsible for regulating our emotions, which include anger, anxiety, mood and irritability; and as these neurotransmitters are responsible for the maintenance of your mood, an imbalance may explain the frustration and rage you may exhibit at times.

Other research has found that early stress during childhood can potentially cause changes in brain development; especially certain brain regions like the hippocampus and amygdale (Teicher et al., 2003).

The hippocampus is responsible for long term memory and the amygdala is where our emotions, for example, fear, is analysed.

Some sufferers from Borderline Personality Disorder have been known to have experienced high levels of stress during their early childhood. It has been felt that this experience may cause changes in early brain development resulting in sufferers acting out their emotions more impulsively than most adults who are more able to control their emotions out of their own free will.

Did you experience high levels of stress during your childhood?

. . . . . . . . . . . . . . . . . . . . . . . . . . . . . . . . . . . . . . . . . . . . . . . . . . . . . . . . . . . . . . . . . . . . . . . . . . . . .

. . . . . . . . . . . . . . . . . . . . . . . . . . . . . . . . . . . . . . . . . . . . . . . . . . . . . . . . . . . . . . . . . . . . . . . . . . . . .

. . . . . . . . . . . . . . . . . . . . . . . . . . . . . . . . . . . . . . . . . . . . . . . . . . . . . . . . . . . . . . . . . . . . . . . . . . . . .

Although researchers are aware of changes in the brain they are still unclear as to whether problems are caused by or are the consequences of the disorder (Leib *et al.*, 2004).

## ▶ DOES THE ENVIRONMENT IN WHICH YOU GREW UP CAUSE YOU TO DEVELOP BORDERLINE PERSONALITY DISORDER?

A number of indicators of someone developing a Borderline Personality Disorder may be due to traumatic experiences whilst they were growing up which include:

- Loss of a loved one either through divorce or bereavement.

- Neglected of their basic needs, for example, love and protection.

- Emotional abuse, for example, criticised or verbally abused.

- Painful illnesses.

- Treated inconsistently by caregiver.

- Exposed to domestic violence.

- Physically abused, for example, beaten.

- Sexually abused by carers they trusted.

- Separated for whatever reason from caregivers or loved ones.

Did you experience any of the above?

. . . . . . . . . . . . . . . . . . . . . . . . . . . . . . . . . . . . . . . . . . . . . . . . . . . . . . . . . . . . . . . . . . . . . . .

. . . . . . . . . . . . . . . . . . . . . . . . . . . . . . . . . . . . . . . . . . . . . . . . . . . . . . . . . . . . . . . . . . . . . . .

. . . . . . . . . . . . . . . . . . . . . . . . . . . . . . . . . . . . . . . . . . . . . . . . . . . . . . . . . . . . . . . . . . . . . . .

. . . . . . . . . . . . . . . . . . . . . . . . . . . . . . . . . . . . . . . . . . . . . . . . . . . . . . . . . . . . . . . . . . . . . . .

Events like those above, which may have happened to you during your early childhood, can have a powerful influence upon your behaviour in later life; this is because these events may have interfered with your emotional growth and your self development.

You are not to blame that these things originally happened to you, but it is up to you now to do all that you can to find a road that leads you to recover from any past experiences that have caused you pain.

Yet, not every child who suffered traumatic experiences has developed Borderline Personality Disorder. There have been some people who have grown up in stable families without any trauma who have developed Borderline Personality Disorder.

So to recap, the causes of your condition are not well understood. It may be the result of:

---

**Chemical imbalance**, that is, Serotonin.

**Developmental changes in the brain**, that is, amygdala and hypothalamus.

**Inherited** from your family.

**Environmental factors**, for example, physical or sexual abuse.

---

But, more likely, it is a combination of the above, hence a person's genetic makeup can make them vulnerable to developing Borderline Personality Disorder, and it is subsequently triggered by environmental events, for example, childhood stresses or abuse.

Having some knowledge of why you have Borderline Personality Disorder can help you to heal and recover, but we can also waste too much time and energy working out the causes when what we need to do is to focus on treatment and believing that recovery is possible. This is much more important!

---

Things for you to remember are that:

---

**You are not to blame for your personality disorder as there are many factors involved which are causing you to think, feel and behave the way you do**

## ▶ WHAT FAMOUS PEOPLE SUFFER FROM BORDERLINE PERSONALITY DISORDER?

Do you know any famous people who may have suffered from Borderline Personality Disorder?

...........................................................................................

...........................................................................................

...........................................................................................

...........................................................................................

Others have speculated that the term Borderline Personality Disorder might apply to well known figures, for example:

■ Actress Marilyn Monroe (Warner, 2007).

■ Author Susanna Kaysen (Everything, 2001) she wrote *'Girl Interrupted'* which is a biography about her hospital experience when suffering from Borderline Personality Disorder, it was also made into a film.

■ Comedian Doug Ferrar (Mattingly & Melisso, 2000).

■ Princess Diana (Bedell Smith, 2000).

The Royal College of Psychiatrists has a booklet on 'Personality Disorder' and is helpful for sufferers and their friends and families and copies can be obtained at the address at end of the workbook.

▶ **End-of-session Questionnaire**

What three important things have you learnt and will take away with you from Session 2 (you may need to browse through this session again to jog your memory).

1 ...................................................................................................................

...................................................................................................................

...................................................................................................................

...................................................................................................................

...................................................................................................................

...................................................................................................................

...................................................................................................................

...................................................................................................................

...................................................................................................................

...................................................................................................................

2 ...................................................................................................................

...................................................................................................................

...................................................................................................................

...................................................................................................................

...................................................................................................................

...................................................................................................................

...................................................................................................................

...................................................................................................................

...................................................................................................................

3 ...................................................................................................................

...................................................................................................................

...................................................................................................................

...................................................................................................................

...................................................................................................................

...................................................................................................................

...................................................................................................................

...................................................................................................................

# Session 3

## ▶ Questionnaire

These questions are not meant to be seen as a test. They are only a means of sharing information and getting you to think about your condition before you start your session. If you are not sure just make a guess; there are no right or wrong answers.

1. What are the symptoms of Borderline Personality Disorder?

2. In what ways do these symptoms affect their lives?

# Session 3

During this session we will be looking at the following commonly asked questions regarding Borderline Personality Disorder.

1. What are the symptoms of Borderline Personality Disorder?

2. What famous people have also self harmed?

# Session 3

> ## WHAT ARE THE SYMPTOMS OF BORDERLINE PERSONALITY DISORDER?

The term Borderline Personality Disorder was originally used in 1938 by Adolf Stern, a psychoanalyst who described his patients as being 'on the borderline between neurosis and psychosis'.

What have you heard about the term 'neurosis'?

. . . . . . . . . . . . . . . . . . . . . . . . . . . . . . . . . . . . . . . . . . . . . . . . . . . . . . . . . . . . . . . . . . . . . . . . . . . . . . . . . . . . . . . .

. . . . . . . . . . . . . . . . . . . . . . . . . . . . . . . . . . . . . . . . . . . . . . . . . . . . . . . . . . . . . . . . . . . . . . . . . . . . . . . . . . . . . . . .

The dictionary defines neurosis as 'a mental disorder which is characterised by exaggerated anxiety and tension' (Bailliere, 1997).

An example of a neurosis condition might be abnormal feelings of anxiety, that someone may need to obsessively check that their doors are locked and also that some people may have phobias.

Do you know of any other abnormal fears that someone might experience if they suffered from neurosis?

. . . . . . . . . . . . . . . . . . . . . . . . . . . . . . . . . . . . . . . . . . . . . . . . . . . . . . . . . . . . . . . . . . . . . . . . . . . . . . . . . . . . . . . .

. . . . . . . . . . . . . . . . . . . . . . . . . . . . . . . . . . . . . . . . . . . . . . . . . . . . . . . . . . . . . . . . . . . . . . . . . . . . . . . . . . . . . . . .

Those suffering from Borderline Personality Disorder may experience abnormal feelings of anxiety.

What have you heard about the term 'psychosis'?

. . . . . . . . . . . . . . . . . . . . . . . . . . . . . . . . . . . . . . . . . . . . . . . . . . . . . . . . . . . . . . . . . . . . . . . . . . . . . . . . . . . . . . . .

. . . . . . . . . . . . . . . . . . . . . . . . . . . . . . . . . . . . . . . . . . . . . . . . . . . . . . . . . . . . . . . . . . . . . . . . . . . . . . . . . . . . . . . .

The dictionary defines psychosis as 'a severe mental disorder in which a sufferer's contact with reality becomes distorted' (Collins, 2001). What this means is that the sufferer's ability to recognise what is real and what is imagined is seriously affected.

Do you know of any symptoms that someone might experience if they suffered from psychosis?

. . . . . . . . . . . . . . . . . . . . . . . . . . . . . . . . . . . . . . . . . . . . . . . . . . . . . . . . . . . . . . . . . . . . . . . . . . . . . . . . . . . . . . . .

. . . . . . . . . . . . . . . . . . . . . . . . . . . . . . . . . . . . . . . . . . . . . . . . . . . . . . . . . . . . . . . . . . . . . . . . . . . . . . . . . . . . . . . .

Those suffering from Borderline Personality Disorder may experience paranoid ideation which is considered a psychosis symptom and will be discussed in more detail in on page 30.

One way of attempting to describe the symptoms of Borderline Personality Disorder is by mnemonically **I DESPAIR:**

**I** Identity disturbance

**D** Dysregulated emotion

**E** Emptiness

**S** Suicidal behaviour

**P** Paranoid ideation

**A** Abandonment

**I** Impulsivity

**R** Rage

(Anzapt, 2007)

Which of the mnemonic I DESPAIR would describe your symptoms?

.................................................................................................................

.................................................................................................................

.................................................................................................................

A sufferer from Borderline Personality Disorder usually becomes noticeable in their adolescence or early adulthood, and if you suffer from this disorder you will find that your beliefs and ways of thinking are not the same as other people, causing much distress to yourself and also other people.

The symptoms of Borderline Personality Disorder usually fall under the following headings. **(Please note that you may not have all of the symptoms):**

## MOOD SWINGS

Please tick all boxes that apply

|  | Yes | No |
|---|---|---|
| I often feel anxious | ☑ | ☐ |
| I often feel low in my mood | ☑ | ☐ |
| I go through cycles of anger and then calm | ☐ | ☐ |

Have you experienced any other feelings that have affected your mood?

. . . . . . . . . . . . . . . . . . . . . . . . . . . . . . . . . . . . . . . . . . . . . . . . . . . . . . . . . . . . . . . . . .

. . . . . . . . . . . . . . . . . . . . . . . . . . . . . . . . . . . . . . . . . . . . . . . . . . . . . . . . . . . . . . . . . .

. . . . . . . . . . . . . . . . . . . . . . . . . . . . . . . . . . . . . . . . . . . . . . . . . . . . . . . . . . . . . . . . . .

If you suffer from Borderline Personality Disorder you may suffer from changeable mood swings, whereby you will feel on top of the world one minute and feel fine and then feel depressed and suicidal the next in a matter of a few hours and for no real reason.

These mood swings can cause you much disruption in your life and prevent you from living a happy, successful life due to your emotions; these emotions may be feelings of anger, frustration, anxiety, guilt and fear which get in the way of you leading a normal life.

If someone gave you a gift right now list all the emotions you think you would feel?

. . . . . . . . . . . . . . . . . . . . . . . . . . . . . . . . . . . . . . . . . . . . . . . . . . . . . . . . . . . . . . . . . .

. . . . . . . . . . . . . . . . . . . . . . . . . . . . . . . . . . . . . . . . . . . . . . . . . . . . . . . . . . . . . . . . . .

. . . . . . . . . . . . . . . . . . . . . . . . . . . . . . . . . . . . . . . . . . . . . . . . . . . . . . . . . . . . . . . . . .

List all the interpretation or understanding that you might have as to why this person gave you the gift?

. . . . . . . . . . . . . . . . . . . . . . . . . . . . . . . . . . . . . . . . . . . . . . . . . . . . . . . . . . . . . . . . . .

. . . . . . . . . . . . . . . . . . . . . . . . . . . . . . . . . . . . . . . . . . . . . . . . . . . . . . . . . . . . . . . . . .

. . . . . . . . . . . . . . . . . . . . . . . . . . . . . . . . . . . . . . . . . . . . . . . . . . . . . . . . . . . . . . . . . .

Describe how your mood might be after experiencing these emotions?

. . . . . . . . . . . . . . . . . . . . . . . . . . . . . . . . . . . . . . . . . . . . . . . . . . . . . . . . . . . . . . . . . .

. . . . . . . . . . . . . . . . . . . . . . . . . . . . . . . . . . . . . . . . . . . . . . . . . . . . . . . . . . . . . . . . . .

Many Borderline Personality Disorder sufferers have difficulty describing their emotions and interpreting the events that led to this emotion. For you to heal, you need to understand how your emotions personally affect you and you also need to let go of any painful emotions that you might have. This will be discussed further in Session 6.

# INTERMITTENT ATTACKS OF PSYCHOTIC EPISODES

*[handwritten:]* i'm going to be exposed / fraud
I'm absolute failure
Self harming is ok . validating

my children
neighbours

Please tick all boxes

|  | Yes | No |
|---|---|---|
| I have had beliefs that have not been shared by others | ✔ | ☐ |
| I think that people don't like me and are against me | ✔ | ☐ |
| People say I misinterpret their behaviour | ✔ | ☐ |

Have you experienced any other symptoms of psychosis that have not been mentioned above?

..........................................................................................................

..........................................................................................................

If you suffer from a borderline personality disorder you may sometimes experience psychotic symptoms for example paranoid ideation; this is feelings of persecution whereby you feel that others are out to harm you in some way. These feelings can last for a few minutes to up to a few hours and usually occur when you are feeling stressed which can cause you to feel that others don't like you or are gossiping about you

Would you say that you have experienced paranoid ideation?

..........................................................................................................

..........................................................................................................

Marsha Lineham (1993) stated that individuals who have experienced stress whilst growing up can have feelings of vulnerability and uncertainty when confronted with stressful situations.

These feelings of paranoia are usually false impressions of situations which you judge to be true rather than a distinct break from reality.

Have you ever felt a bit 'out of it' like you are daydreaming or felt like you are just going through the motions or 'running on automatic'?

..........................................................................................................

..........................................................................................................

This feeling is called dissociation and is a type of coping mechanism which helps to protect sufferers from difficult feelings or stressful situations.

'Dissociation is a common and healthy defence used in response to life-threatening danger and is associated with memory loss and a sense of disconnection from yourself or your surroundings' (Dissociation World, 2007).

# IMPULSIVE ACTION PATTERNS

Please tick all boxes that apply

|  | Yes | No |
|---|---|---|
| I binge eat | ✔ | ☐ |
| I have sped fast in cars | ☐ | ☐ |
| I have misused illicit drugs | ☐ | ☐ |
| I have misused alcohol | ✔ | ☐ |
| I have had many casual sexual relationships | ✔ | ☐ |
| I overspend and ~~have huge~~ debts | ✔ | ☐ |
| I have gambled a lot of money | ☐ | ☐ |

Are there any other impulsive behaviours not mentioned that you have experienced?

..........................................................................................

..........................................................................................

This symptom can cause you terrible problems and you may do these things because you are trying to deal with emotional pain or emptiness.

You may feel that alcohol, drugs, overspending, overeating and casual sex provide you with a quick fix because they can alter your mood and these impulsive behaviours may also help you to escape from some of your unbearable feelings such as worthlessness and loneliness.

Is this true for you, if so how do the above behaviours help you cope?

*Takes away the empitiness & being*

..........................................................................................

..........................................................................................

Most people are able to control their impulses and delay immediate gratification because they are aware of long term consequences for example:

- weight gain
- unplanned pregnancies
- sexually transmitted diseases
- motor car accidents
- physical fights
- physical conditions, for example, liver problems
- debt collectors
- criminal record.

Have you suffered from some of the above consequences due to your impulsive behaviour?

*Chronic fatigue*

..........................................................................................

..........................................................................................

But those suffering from Borderline Personality Disorder find it hard to control these impulses because when they feel anxious or empty inside these activities are an appreciated distraction.

Also, these behaviours could be seen as a kind of self destruction or self hate and the wish behind these behaviours maybe is to bring about some form of rescue from others. There are ways of coping with these difficult feelings which will be discussed further in Session 6.

## CHRONIC FEELINGS OF EMPTINESS AND BOREDOM

Please tick all boxes

| | Yes | No |
|---|---|---|
| I constantly feel restless | ☑ | ☐ |
| I am always feeling bored | ☑ | ☐ |
| I feel really scared about being on my own | ☑ | ☐ |
| I feel confused when others are around | ☑ | ☐ |
| I constantly have feelings of emptiness | ☑ | ☐ |
| I will go to any lengths not to be alone | ☐ | ☐ |

Are there any other feelings that you have experienced which relate to your life having no meaning or purpose which has not been mentioned above?

..........................................................................................................

..........................................................................................................

..........................................................................................................

Emptiness can be described as being unable to feel anything emotionally.

Would this best describe how you feel?

..........................................................................................................

..........................................................................................................

..........................................................................................................

Boredom can be described as being uninterested and knowing that you must do something but don't know what. Otto Fenichel (1951) described boredom as a sort of emotional withdrawing.

Would this best describe how you feel?

..........................................................................................................

..........................................................................................................

..........................................................................................................

You may find it difficult to comfort yourself when you are alone, but in Session 6 it will be discussed further, along with ways of learning to feel comfortable when you are on your own.

# SUICIDE BEHAVIOUR

Please tick all boxes that apply

|  | Yes | No |
|---|---|---|
| I have attempted to take my life | ✔ | ☐ |
| I have made suicidal threats on occasions | ✔ | ☐ |
| I don't necessarily want to die but to escape from my situation | ✔ | ☐ |

Which other feelings have you gone through which relate to your suicide ideation?

.................................................................................

.................................................................................

.................................................................................

Those who suffer from Borderline Personality Disorder often make suicidal gestures; it is very important to know to whom you can turn for support. This will be discussed further in Session 6 and important telephone numbers are available at the end of this workbook.

# GREAT FEAR OF ABANDONMENT

Please tick all boxes that apply

|  | Yes | No |
|---|---|---|
| I will do anything to stop people I love from leaving me | ✔ | ☐ |
| I fear people will eventually abandon me | ✔ | ☐ |
| I keep asking my partner if they are going to leave me | ☐ | ☐ |
| I am terrified of being rejected | ✔ | ☐ |
| I rely a lot on others for emotional support | ✔ | ☐ |
| I rely a lot on others to make decisions for me | ✔ | ☐ |
| I fear disapproval from others | ✔ | ☐ |

Are there any other feelings that you have experienced which relate to you being neglected or feel that you may be left behind?

.................................................................................

.................................................................................

.................................................................................

Inside our memory there is what's called an 'inner child', this is the little girl or boy we used to be, whose wish is to be loved and cared for. It is the emotional part of us where our feelings live. If, for whatever reason, our 'inner child' was not allowed to mature in a safe and healthy way it can cause you to become disconnected with your feelings which can cause much confusion for you.

Those who suffer from Borderline Personality Disorder have a very strong fear of being lonely and are terrified of being rejected because this child part has been left alone either emotionally or physically in some way when they were growing up; and it is this part of the self who is craving for extra attention and reassurance that they are safe and wanted.

Do you feel that your 'inner child' is screaming out to be loved and cared for?

. . . . . . . . . . . . . . . . . . . . . . . . . . . . . . . . . . . . . . . . . . . . . . . . . . . . . . . . . . . . . . . . . . . . . . . . . . .

. . . . . . . . . . . . . . . . . . . . . . . . . . . . . . . . . . . . . . . . . . . . . . . . . . . . . . . . . . . . . . . . . . . . . . . . . . .

. . . . . . . . . . . . . . . . . . . . . . . . . . . . . . . . . . . . . . . . . . . . . . . . . . . . . . . . . . . . . . . . . . . . . . . . . . .

It was not your fault what happened to you when you were growing up, but it is your responsibility as an adult to do all you can to take care of your 'inner child'. In Session 6 we will be looking at ways on how you can do this.

## RELATIONSHIP PROBLEMS

Please tick all boxes that apply

|  | Yes | No |
| --- | --- | --- |
| I cannot tolerate uncertainty | ☑ | ☐ |
| I have a history of stormy relationships | ☐ | ☐ |
| I have had difficulties with people I work with | ☐ | ☐ |
| I can form an immediate attachment to someone | ☐ | ☐ |
| People are either good or bad with nothing in between | ☐ | ☐ |
| I have been known to blame others for my situation | ☐ | ☐ |

What other experiences or feelings have you experienced which have caused you problems when dealing with other people?

. . . . . . . . . . . . . . . . . . . . . . . . . . . . . . . . . . . . . . . . . . . . . . . . . . . . . . . . . . . . . . . . . . . . . . . . . . .

. . . . . . . . . . . . . . . . . . . . . . . . . . . . . . . . . . . . . . . . . . . . . . . . . . . . . . . . . . . . . . . . . . . . . . . . . . .

If you suffer from Borderline Personality Disorder you will find that you are hypersensitive to the cues in your environment and react to them with an unpredictable set of emotions and behaviours.

People who suffer from your disorder have main thoughts which rely on what is happening in their relationships at this present moment. Because you may have difficulty not knowing 'who you are' and underneath this feeling is the fear that you may be rejected or abandoned, you might try and search out your identity through other people. Your need for love and acceptance may cause you to fear that if you lost this relationship you might lose an inner sense of who you are.

Would you say this was true for you?

. . . . . . . . . . . . . . . . . . . . . . . . . . . . . . . . . . . . . . . . . . . . . . . . . . . . . . . . . . . . . . . . . . . . . . . . . . .

. . . . . . . . . . . . . . . . . . . . . . . . . . . . . . . . . . . . . . . . . . . . . . . . . . . . . . . . . . . . . . . . . . . . . . . . . . .

Since abandonment causes you to feel emptiness you will try and prevent it from happening it at all costs.

Defence mechanisms are psychological strategies that help individuals to minimise anxiety. A common defence mechanism that those with Borderline Personality Disorder use to protect themselves from anxiety is called 'splitting'.

To describe splitting is when, as children, we separate our world by things being either all good or all bad and we are unable to comprehend that things can change from minute to minute and that someone can be both good and bad.

Sufferers of Borderline Personality Disorder also experience this perception of splitting; this is due to their childhood development being disrupted by difficulties whilst they were growing up. It is impossible for them to appreciate the grey areas of life in the same way that other adults can. This is explored further in Session 6.

## SELF HARM

Please tick all boxes that apply

| | Yes | No |
|---|---|---|
| I have hurt myself when I feel stressed | ☑ | ☐ |
| I feel guilty and bad after I have hurt myself | ☑ | ☑ |
| Self harm gives me a sense of relief | ☑ | ☐ |
| Hurting myself is triggered by a feeling that I can't cope | ☑ | ☐ |
| When I self harm I don't necessarily want to die | ☑ | ☐ |

What other feelings and emotions have you gone through which relate to your self harming behaviour?

. . . . . . . . . . . . . . . . . . . . . . . . . . . . . . . . . . . . . . . . . . . . . . . . . . . . . . . . . . . . . . . . . . . . . . . . . . . . . . . . . . . . . . . . . . . . . . . . . . . . . . . . . . . . . . . . . . . . . . . . . . . . . . . . . . . . . . . . . . . . . . . . . . . . . . . . . . . . . . . . . . . . . . . . . . . . . . . . . . . . . . . . . . . . . . . . . . . . . . . . . . . . . . . . . . . . . . . . . . .

Some of the types of self harming behaviours are:

■ cutting
■ burning
■ excessive scratching
■ hitting yourself.

Self harming behaviour has often been mistaken for a suicide attempt, but most people who self harm will tell you that their intention is not to die, but that they have become caught up in what some describe as a distressing act which is their way of dealing with difficult feelings.

Dusty Miller (1994) stated that there is so much meaning behind the act of self harm and those who are drawn into it are not always aware of the reasons why they do.

If you self harm, do you understand the reasons why?

. . . . . . . . . . . . . . . . . . . . . . . . . . . . . . . . . . . . . . . . . . . . . . . . . . . . . . . . . . . . . . . . . . . . . . . . . . . . . . . . . . . . . . . . . . . . . . . . . . . . . . . . . . . . . . . . . . . . . . . . . . . . . . . . . . . . . . . . . . . . . . . . . . . . . . . . . . . . . . . . . . . . . . . . . . . . . . . . . . . . . . . . . . . . . . . . . . . . . . . . . . . . . . . . . . . . . . . . . . .

Some of the meanings behind self harming actions are:

- coping strategy

- way of expressing anger

- cry for help

- acts as a distraction

**Coping strategy**

Have you felt tremendously stressed about something that was bothering you and did not know how to deal with the problem?

..................................................................................................
..................................................................................................

Did it get to the stage whereby these feelings of fear and worry overwhelmed you and you felt like you were unable to cope with anything around you?

..................................................................................................
..................................................................................................

Did these feelings trigger the need to do whatever it took to get the situation under control and restore a sense of calm and to relieve your distress?

..................................................................................................
..................................................................................................

**A way of expressing anger**

Some sufferers manage anger by self harming. They have a wish to punish another person, but mainly they want to punish themselves for some of the wrongs that have happened to them in their life, whether they were responsible or not which for some sufferers continues the abusive patterns from their past.

**A cry for help**

A common myth of self harm is that it is an attention-seeking behaviour.

How do you feel about this myth?

..................................................................................................
..................................................................................................

But the truth is that most sufferers would prefer not to self harm and are very self conscious of their scars and will do anything to hide their behaviour from others. Having said that, seeking attention is a normal human basic need and we have to understand why a person would go to such lengths to get the care they need.

What most sufferers would say is that they want to show others that they are hurting inside but don't have the words which would communicate the emotional pain they are going through. So for them to ask for the help and attention they so desperately need, they may attempt to invite others to intervene and rescue them from their unbearable feelings. This act is usually triggered by feelings of rejection, self hatred and anger.

**Acts as a distraction**

Have you experienced a feeling of emptiness and a sense of numbness where you felt disconnected from the real world in some way?

. . . . . . . . . . . . . . . . . . . . . . . . . . . . . . . . . . . . . . . . . . . . . . . . . . . . . . . . . . . . . . . . . . . . . . . . . . . . .

. . . . . . . . . . . . . . . . . . . . . . . . . . . . . . . . . . . . . . . . . . . . . . . . . . . . . . . . . . . . . . . . . . . . . . . . . . . . .

Your brain copes with bad memories by blocking out distressful feelings causing you to feel lost, alone and detached from your emotions. The act of self harm can make you feel alive again and reconnecting you to the real world.

Seeking relief from emotional pain by being distracted by physical pain is one way of dealing with these feelings. Also it has been said that the act of self harm releases endorphins, the 'feel good' chemicals in our brain which provide comfort for emotional distress as well as being the body's natural painkillers.

## ▶ WHAT FAMOUS PEOPLE HAVE SELF HARMED

There have been stories in the media regarding famous people who have been known to self harm (Gabrielle, 2007):

- Johnny Depp (actor)
- Princess Diana
- Angelina Jolie (actress)
- Kelly Holmes (gold medallist)
- Marilyn Manson (singer).

How do you feel about the above famous people using self harming behaviours to cope with difficult emotions?

. . . . . . . . . . . . . . . . . . . . . . . . . . . . . . . . . . . . . . . . . . . . . . . . . . . . . . . . . . . . . . . . . . . . . . . . . . . . .

. . . . . . . . . . . . . . . . . . . . . . . . . . . . . . . . . . . . . . . . . . . . . . . . . . . . . . . . . . . . . . . . . . . . . . . . . . . . .

. . . . . . . . . . . . . . . . . . . . . . . . . . . . . . . . . . . . . . . . . . . . . . . . . . . . . . . . . . . . . . . . . . . . . . . . . . . . .

Some of the above celebrities have worked through their difficult emotions and do not have the need to hurt themselves anymore. This is not an easy habit to break though, and if self harming remains a way of coping for you there is more discussion on this struggle in Session 6.

## ANGER

Please tick all boxes that apply

|  | Yes | No |
|---|---|---|
| I have difficulty controlling my temper | ☐ | ☐ |
| I have uncontrollable rages about minor events | ☐ | ☐ |
| I have committed a crime due to my anger | ☐ | ☐ |

What other experiences or feelings have you experienced which relate to your anger?

..................................................................................................

..................................................................................................

Anger is a normal emotion and is part of being a human being. It can be a good thing to have because it tells us when we are getting into physically or emotionally unsafe circumstances. Anger is only a problem when it gets out of balance, which can be destructive to ourselves and others.

Those who suffer from Borderline Personality Disorder feel all emotions intensely, especially anger. It can often be triggered by minor incidents and can come without any warning.

**Triggers that may cause you to feel angry:**

- You are experiencing emotional pain, for example, disappointment or abandonment.
- You are frustrated due to something you cannot have.
- Stress is causing you to be nervous about a situation.
- You feel attacked, unfairly criticised or shamed by someone.
- You might be experiencing physical pain.
- You might be feeling vulnerable in your emotions.
- Someone might make fun of you.
- Craving for illicit drugs or alcohol.
- You think that you may lose some choices and may want to control the situation.

What events have triggered your anger in the past?

..................................................................................................

..................................................................................................

..................................................................................................

**Understanding what aggravated your feelings of anger:**

- Feeling that someone has hurt your feelings.
- You are testing your family or others as to whether they care about you.
- You fear that you may lose the love of someone you care about.

- You hit out first before they do.
- You demand the attention you so desperately crave for.
- You want revenge.
- You have strong feelings of hatred.
- You may have feelings of jealousy.
- You feel betrayed.
- You feel overwhelmed by feelings from your past, for example, guilt.
- You feel misunderstood.
- You feel that you have been lied to.
- You feel rejected or left out.
- You feel afraid and anxious.

What feelings have provoked your feelings of anger?

.................................................................................................
.................................................................................................
.................................................................................................

**Going through the feelings of your anger:**

- Your muscles tighten up.
- You want to throw something or hit someone.
- You have a feeling of being out of control.
- You feel dizzy and light-headed.
- Your face feels flushed and your heart beats very fast.
- Your speech is faster and more intense.
- You might keep your anger buried inside which causes your head or stomach to ache.
- You will manipulate your needs through your anger.
- You want to cry.

What physical or emotional experiences have you felt when you have been angry?

.................................................................................................
.................................................................................................
.................................................................................................

**How you communicate your anger:**

- You may hit someone or something.
- You may shout and be verbally abusive.
- You may withdraw from contact with others.
- You may throw things around.
- You make threatening gestures.
- You may get involved in a physical fight with someone.
- You may self harm.

- You may make suicidal gestures.
- You may slam doors.

What behaviour have you acted out when angry?

.....................................................................................................

.....................................................................................................

.....................................................................................................

### The results of your anger

- You feel unable to concentrate.
- It causes you to feel frightened.
- It causes you to feel shame.
- Alienates you from your loved ones.
- Causes you to detach yourself from your feelings.
- You feel remorseful and guilty.
- Can cause you to have a criminal record and a prison sentence.
- Can be seen as a trigger to abuse alcohol or illicit drugs to cope with difficult feelings.
- Damages your reputation.
- Feeling of punishing yourself and others.
- Can ruin your peace of mind.
- Cause problems with your career.
- Spoils relationship with your loved ones.
- Damage your health.

What have been some of the after effects of your anger?

.....................................................................................................

.....................................................................................................

.....................................................................................................

You, in all probability, don't like feeling that you are letting your emotions control you, but you need to understand these feelings of anger can also control your life.

It is impossible to get rid of anger from our lives as we will always run into situations which arouse our anger, especially those who suffer from Borderline Personality Disorder due to their intense emotions. It is equally OK to feel angry, but it is how you express this anger that is important.

The key approach to handling your anger is first to recognise that you have an anger problem and then for you to take responsibility for:

- The problems that you have caused for yourself due to your angry outbursts
- To address angry feelings with new ways of coping with difficult feelings and situations.

A problem for most who suffer from Borderline Personality Disorder is that the coping mechanism that is used to protect them and help them through each day stops them from taking responsibility for their feelings and actions. You need to find other ways of letting out your anger without hurting yourself or others and in Session 6 this will be discussed further.

**SELF IDENTITY**

|  | Please tick all boxes that apply |
|---|---|
|  | Yes No |
| I find it difficult to verbalise my feelings | ☐ ☐ |
| I am not fulfilling my intellectual potential | ☑ ☐ |
| I feel evil and bad | ☑ ☐ |
| I am unable to discipline myself e.g. stick to a diet | ☑ ☐ |
| I feel shame and guilt | ☑ ☐ |
| I feel ugly and unattractive | ☑ ☐ |
| I feel lost and find it difficult to trust people | ☑ ☐ |
| I hate myself and think others hate me too | ☑ ☐ |
| I feel that whatever I do is not good enough | ☑ ☐ |
| I crave approval from others | ☑ ☐ |

Are there any other problems about how you see yourself that have not been mentioned above?

. . . . . . . . . . . . . . . . . . . . . . . . . . . . . . . . . . . . . . . . . . . . . . . . . . . . . . . . . . . . . . . . . . . . . . . . . . . . . . . . .

. . . . . . . . . . . . . . . . . . . . . . . . . . . . . . . . . . . . . . . . . . . . . . . . . . . . . . . . . . . . . . . . . . . . . . . . . . . . . . . . .

Do you know who you really are? Describe in your own words what it feels like to be you:

. . . . . . . . . . . . . . . . . . . . . . . . . . . . . . . . . . . . . . . . . . . . . . . . . . . . . . . . . . . . . . . . . . . . . . . . . . . . . . . . .

. . . . . . . . . . . . . . . . . . . . . . . . . . . . . . . . . . . . . . . . . . . . . . . . . . . . . . . . . . . . . . . . . . . . . . . . . . . . . . . . .

. . . . . . . . . . . . . . . . . . . . . . . . . . . . . . . . . . . . . . . . . . . . . . . . . . . . . . . . . . . . . . . . . . . . . . . . . . . . . . . . .

Those suffering from Borderline Personality Disorder do not usually have a sense of their own identities and feel detached or dissociated from their true self.

Some sufferers think that whatever their identity is, they feel they will never be good enough. For example, someone with a Borderline Personality Disorder might consider herself attractive, but then if they see a woman who she feels is nice-looking, she then thinks she is ugly again.

Those suffering from this disorder feel that whatever their self is they will never be acceptable; this is because they judge themselves too harshly and that their self esteem can only be obtained by pleasing others; this will be discussed further in Session 6.

## ▶ End-of-session Questionnaire

What three important things have you learnt and will take away with you from Session 3 (you may need to browse through this session again to jog your memory).

1 ...........................................................................................................

...........................................................................................................

...........................................................................................................

...........................................................................................................

...........................................................................................................

...........................................................................................................

...........................................................................................................

...........................................................................................................

...........................................................................................................

...........................................................................................................

2 ...........................................................................................................

...........................................................................................................

...........................................................................................................

...........................................................................................................

...........................................................................................................

...........................................................................................................

...........................................................................................................

...........................................................................................................

...........................................................................................................

...........................................................................................................

3 ...........................................................................................................

...........................................................................................................

...........................................................................................................

...........................................................................................................

...........................................................................................................

...........................................................................................................

...........................................................................................................

...........................................................................................................

# Session 4

► **Questionnaire**

These questions are not meant to be seen as a test. They are only a means of sharing information and getting you to think about your condition before you start your session. If you are not sure just make a guess; there are no right or wrong answers.

1. What are talking therapies?

2. What is the difference between a psychologist and a psychiatrist?

# Session 4

During this session we will be looking at the following commonly asked questions regarding Borderline Personality Disorder:

1. What are talking therapies?
2. What are creative arts therapies?
3. What are the roles of professionals who treat me?
4. What difficulties might I anticipate regarding a working relationship with my therapist?

# Session 4

## ▶ WHAT ARE TALKING THERAPIES?

Talking therapies or psychological therapies involve talking to a trained therapist about how your condition affects you. Talking treatments are a central part of treatment for sufferers of Borderline Personality Disorder and is more effective than medication, although medication can work alongside talking therapies if needed.

Most psychotherapeutic approaches focus on exploring sufferer's emotions, thoughts and behaviours and during therapy you would be encouraged to let go of the past and work on the here and now; there may be times when you experience feelings of anxiety or anger.

What feelings have you experienced whilst working with your therapist?

..........................................................................................

..........................................................................................

..........................................................................................

Talking therapies may at times cause you to feel vulnerable and afraid, but with the support of your therapist you will learn how to tolerate your pain and understand why you are the way you are. It is felt that if you feel the pain and work through it, you will slowly begin to knock down the walls that you have built up high around you.

A therapist will help you learn the skills and tools to do this but be prepared for the times when you go one step forward and two steps backward; don't worry, this is part of your recovery.

You have to really believe that change can happen and that your life could be more meaningful, but if you don't start those first steps to recovery your pain will continue and worsen if you don't take that journey.

Do you feel ready to take that journey?

..........................................................................................

..........................................................................................

..........................................................................................

There is a range of talking therapies that are known to be helpful in treating Borderline Personality Disorders and they include:

- psychodynamic therapy
- dialectic behavioural therapy
- cognitive behavioural therapy
- schema therapy
- cognitive analytical therapy

■ therapeutic community

■ family therapy

■ support groups.

There is also a range of creative arts therapies that are known to be helpful in treating Borderline Personality Disorders and they include:

■ art therapy

■ drama therapy

■ psychodrama therapy.

These will be discussed in more detail below.

## PSYCHODYNAMIC THERAPY

Psychodynamic therapy helps sufferers to understand their difficult emotions more fully. During this treatment sufferers will explore past experiences, usually childhood, and understand the impact these may have had on their personality development.

One aspect of psychodynamic therapy is called 'object relations' which relates to 'the emotional bond that people form . . . 'the capacity to form loving relationships with other people', Dictionary of Psychology (2001). Object relations explore sufferers' emotional states of attachment, frustration and rejection.

Foelsch and Kernberg (1998) theory of 'Transference Focused Psychotherapy' explores the relationship between the therapist and sufferer and focuses on the 'here and now' relying less on the past experiences of the sufferer.

The above theories have been seen to be helpful in treating those who suffer from Borderline Personality Disorder.

Have you had any psychodynamic therapy?

. . . . . . . . . . . . . . . . . . . . . . . . . . . . . . . . . . . . . . . . . . . . . . . . . . . . . . . . . . . . . . . . . . . . . . . . . . . . . . . . . . . . . . . . . . .

. . . . . . . . . . . . . . . . . . . . . . . . . . . . . . . . . . . . . . . . . . . . . . . . . . . . . . . . . . . . . . . . . . . . . . . . . . . . . . . . . . . . . . . . . . .

If so was it helpful or not and why?

. . . . . . . . . . . . . . . . . . . . . . . . . . . . . . . . . . . . . . . . . . . . . . . . . . . . . . . . . . . . . . . . . . . . . . . . . . . . . . . . . . . . . . . . . . .

. . . . . . . . . . . . . . . . . . . . . . . . . . . . . . . . . . . . . . . . . . . . . . . . . . . . . . . . . . . . . . . . . . . . . . . . . . . . . . . . . . . . . . . . . . .

If you have not had this type of therapy would you be interested?

. . . . . . . . . . . . . . . . . . . . . . . . . . . . . . . . . . . . . . . . . . . . . . . . . . . . . . . . . . . . . . . . . . . . . . . . . . . . . . . . . . . . . . . . . . .

. . . . . . . . . . . . . . . . . . . . . . . . . . . . . . . . . . . . . . . . . . . . . . . . . . . . . . . . . . . . . . . . . . . . . . . . . . . . . . . . . . . . . . . . . . .

The goal of psychodynamic therapy is to help sufferers to work through their painful feelings within a safe environment with a therapist who understands them and with whom they have developed some trust. This type of therapy can be quite time consuming with sessions of a minimum of once a week for one to two years or longer.

# DIALECTIC BEHAVIOURAL THERAPY

Dialectic Behavioural Therapy (DBT) was developed in the 1990s by Dr Marsha Lineham and her therapy focuses on helping sufferers of Borderline Personality Disorder to develop new skills on how to manage their difficult emotions and behaviours (Lineham, 2003).

There are four main skills that are the central part to this therapy and they concentrate on:

- *Mindfulness*
- This skill helps sufferers to focus on something else other than their distressing thoughts, by remaining calm and 'staying in the moment'.

- *Emotional regulation*
- This skill helps sufferers to identify their emotions and explores how these emotions affect their lives; it also teaches sufferers how to look after themselves.

- *Distress tolerance*
- This skill helps sufferers learn how to cope with life's crisis's, which include distractions, and on how to self soothe.

- *Interpersonal effectiveness*
- This skill teaches sufferers about self respect and how to improve relationships.

Have you had any dialectic behavioural therapy?

. . . . . . . . . . . . . . . . . . . . . . . . . . . . . . . . . . . . . . . . . . . . . . . . . . . . . . . . . . . . . . . . . . . . . . . . . . . . . . . . . .

. . . . . . . . . . . . . . . . . . . . . . . . . . . . . . . . . . . . . . . . . . . . . . . . . . . . . . . . . . . . . . . . . . . . . . . . . . . . . . . . . .

If so was it helpful or not and why?

. . . . . . . . . . . . . . . . . . . . . . . . . . . . . . . . . . . . . . . . . . . . . . . . . . . . . . . . . . . . . . . . . . . . . . . . . . . . . . . . . .

. . . . . . . . . . . . . . . . . . . . . . . . . . . . . . . . . . . . . . . . . . . . . . . . . . . . . . . . . . . . . . . . . . . . . . . . . . . . . . . . . .

If you have not had this type of therapy would you be interested in trying it?

. . . . . . . . . . . . . . . . . . . . . . . . . . . . . . . . . . . . . . . . . . . . . . . . . . . . . . . . . . . . . . . . . . . . . . . . . . . . . . . . . .

. . . . . . . . . . . . . . . . . . . . . . . . . . . . . . . . . . . . . . . . . . . . . . . . . . . . . . . . . . . . . . . . . . . . . . . . . . . . . . . . . .

Dialectic behavioural therapy consists of weekly individual psychotherapy, group skills training, telephone consultation and weekly meetings. This type of therapy is known to be a successful and effective treatment for Borderline Personality Disorder sufferers. Like most therapies for Borderline Personality Disorder the treatment lasts for at least a year or more.

# COGNITIVE BEHAVIOURAL THERAPY

Aaron T. Beck (1964) is the founder of Cognitive Behavioural Therapy (CBT) and his theory identifies how people think and feel and how it has an affect on their behaviour.

For example, if you had an unhelpful negative thought this in turn would affect your mood, perhaps causing you to feel low in yourself and you may respond by behaving in an unhelpful way, e.g. self harm or arguments with friends and family.

Have you had any cognitive behavioural therapy?

...................................................................................................

...................................................................................................

If so was it helpful or not and why?

...................................................................................................

...................................................................................................

If you have not had this type of therapy would you be interested in trying it?

...................................................................................................

...................................................................................................

Cognitive behavioural therapy consists of a set amount of weekly sessions and with your therapist you will work together looking at your thoughts, feelings and behaviour and whether they are helpful or unhelpful to you. You will also be given 'homework' to practice new coping skills learnt in therapy.

Cognitive behavioural therapy has been helpful in treating Borderline Personality Disorder sufferers because small changes in one area, e.g. thoughts and feelings, can lead to changes in other areas, e.g. behaviour.

## SCHEMA THERAPY

Jeffrey Young (1994) developed Schema Therapy and this therapy focuses on recognising and changing the 'early maladaptive schemas' that are thought to underpin the origins of Borderline Personality Disorder.

Young stated that schema's are 'beliefs and feelings about oneself and the environment which the individual accepts without questioning.

If your belief about yourself as a child was 'I am no good' due to criticism from teachers, parents and others you would carry this schema or belief about yourself into your adulthood.

Young and his colleague Bricker (1993) found 18 different schemas, but we will only mention a few:

- Emotional deprivation – this is a belief that your emotional needs will never be met by others and you may say to yourself 'people don't care about me'.
- Abandonment – this is a belief that you will lose anyone with whom you form an attachment and you may say to yourself 'people will leave me'.
- Mistrust – this is a belief that you expect others to hurt you and may say to yourself 'I anticipate others will hurt me'.

- Social undesirability – this is a belief that you are unattractive and you may say to yourself 'I am ugly'.
- Self sacrifice – this is a belief that you must sacrifice your needs to help others and you may say to yourself 'I am unimportant'.

The goal of schema therapy is to weaken the schemas and identify strategies on how to deal with them.

Have you had any schema therapy?

. . . . . . . . . . . . . . . . . . . . . . . . . . . . . . . . . . . . . . . . . . . . . . . . . . . . . . . . . . . . . . . . . . . . . . . . . . . . . . . . . . . . . . . . . . . . . .

. . . . . . . . . . . . . . . . . . . . . . . . . . . . . . . . . . . . . . . . . . . . . . . . . . . . . . . . . . . . . . . . . . . . . . . . . . . . . . . . . . . . . . . . . . . . . .

If so was it helpful or not and why?

. . . . . . . . . . . . . . . . . . . . . . . . . . . . . . . . . . . . . . . . . . . . . . . . . . . . . . . . . . . . . . . . . . . . . . . . . . . . . . . . . . . . . . . . . . . . . .

. . . . . . . . . . . . . . . . . . . . . . . . . . . . . . . . . . . . . . . . . . . . . . . . . . . . . . . . . . . . . . . . . . . . . . . . . . . . . . . . . . . . . . . . . . . . . .

If you have not had this type of therapy would you be interested in trying it?

. . . . . . . . . . . . . . . . . . . . . . . . . . . . . . . . . . . . . . . . . . . . . . . . . . . . . . . . . . . . . . . . . . . . . . . . . . . . . . . . . . . . . . . . . . . . . .

. . . . . . . . . . . . . . . . . . . . . . . . . . . . . . . . . . . . . . . . . . . . . . . . . . . . . . . . . . . . . . . . . . . . . . . . . . . . . . . . . . . . . . . . . . . . . .

## COGNITIVE ANALYTIC THERAPY

Anthony Ryle developed Cognitive Analytic Therapy (CAT) during the 1980s and his theory focuses on understanding unhelpful patterns of behaviour that cause individuals problems and finding alternative helpful strategies on how to cope with their emotional difficulties.

Have you had any cognitive analytic therapy?

. . . . . . . . . . . . . . . . . . . . . . . . . . . . . . . . . . . . . . . . . . . . . . . . . . . . . . . . . . . . . . . . . . . . . . . . . . . . . . . . . . . . . . . . . . . . . .

. . . . . . . . . . . . . . . . . . . . . . . . . . . . . . . . . . . . . . . . . . . . . . . . . . . . . . . . . . . . . . . . . . . . . . . . . . . . . . . . . . . . . . . . . . . . . .

If so was it helpful or not and why?

. . . . . . . . . . . . . . . . . . . . . . . . . . . . . . . . . . . . . . . . . . . . . . . . . . . . . . . . . . . . . . . . . . . . . . . . . . . . . . . . . . . . . . . . . . . . . .

. . . . . . . . . . . . . . . . . . . . . . . . . . . . . . . . . . . . . . . . . . . . . . . . . . . . . . . . . . . . . . . . . . . . . . . . . . . . . . . . . . . . . . . . . . . . . .

If you have not had this type of therapy would you be interested in trying it?

. . . . . . . . . . . . . . . . . . . . . . . . . . . . . . . . . . . . . . . . . . . . . . . . . . . . . . . . . . . . . . . . . . . . . . . . . . . . . . . . . . . . . . . . . . . . . .

. . . . . . . . . . . . . . . . . . . . . . . . . . . . . . . . . . . . . . . . . . . . . . . . . . . . . . . . . . . . . . . . . . . . . . . . . . . . . . . . . . . . . . . . . . . . . .

Cognitive analytical therapy consists of a set amount of weekly sessions and involves you and your therapist working together to look at what has hindered you from your past and to explore alternative ways in which you can move forward into the present.

Cognitive analytical therapy has helped sufferers of Borderline Personality Disorder to recognise unhelpful relationship patterns that have continued through their lives but which they find difficult to change without help.

## THERAPEUTIC COMMUNITIES

Maxwell Jones developed the concept of therapeutic communities and established the reputable Henderson Hospital in 1947 which pioneered treatment for sufferers of Borderline Personality Disorder.

Some principles of therapeutic communities are:

- To encourage independence.
- To create a sense of belonging.
- For staff and residents to share responsibility for any decisions that are made within community affairs, including who will be admitted to the unit.
- To keep communication open with all information shared by everyone.
- To maintain a non judgemental attitude towards others within the therapeutic community.

Treatment is usually voluntary but stresses the importance of staff and residents working together in running the unit. Part of this treatment is talking about your feelings to the group, this may be hard for you to begin with, but it would also be very helpful.

Have you been admitted to a therapeutic community?

...........................................................................................

...........................................................................................

If so was it helpful or not and why?

...........................................................................................

...........................................................................................

## FAMILY THERAPY

Gregory Bateson laid down the foundations of Family Therapy around the 1960s in which the family system as a whole, and not just one person, is treated.

Family therapy helps by educating those who care about you on your Borderline Personality Disorder. This will help improve family communication and this therapy will also provide support for both you and your family.

Family therapists are usually specifically trained in this type of psychotherapy and would be helpful to sufferers because this type of treatment stresses the importance of family relationships as a major factor in recovery.

Family therapy can take place in a family home, or more commonly in a hospital or clinic.

Have you had any family therapy?

......................................................................................

......................................................................................

If so was it helpful or not and why?

......................................................................................

......................................................................................

If you have not had this type of therapy would you be interested in trying it?

......................................................................................

......................................................................................

Some therapist use an eclectic approach to treatment, this means combining approaches from psychodynamic, cognitive behavioural therapy and also dialectic behavioural therapy.

## ▶ WHAT ARE CREATIVE ARTS THERAPIES?

Creative arts therapy includes: art therapy, drama therapy and psychodrama therapy and it is used to express difficult emotions.

Sufferers can sometimes find it difficult to address their painful emotions in words, but may find it easier and less threatening to express themselves through either art or drama.

### ART THERAPY

Art therapy is a form of psychotherapy and Margaret Naumburg and Edith Kramer (Ballou, 1995) are considered to be the founders of this type of therapy. It not about learning art techniques and you don't need to be artistic to be able to take part in this treatment, but it is about helping sufferers to explore their innermost thoughts and feelings without using words.

Benefits of art therapy include:

■ It helps you to discover the real you.
■ It can build up your confidence.
■ It allows you to express emotions that you find difficult to verbalise.
■ It relieves stress.

Art therapy tools include:

■ chalk
■ crayons
■ collage
■ finger paints

■ plasticine

■ clay.

Have you had any art therapy?

.................................................................................................

.................................................................................................

If so was it helpful or not and why?

.................................................................................................

.................................................................................................

If you have not had this type of therapy would you be interested in trying it?

.................................................................................................

.................................................................................................

Art therapy can take place as part of an inpatient or outpatient treatment programme

## DRAMA THERAPY

During the 1940s Peter Slade was Britain's first drama therapist and influenced the work of Sue Jennings who introduced drama workshops in psychiatric hospitals during the 1960s and 1970s. Drama therapists usually have a qualification in creative arts and have taken on extra training in psychology and psychotherapy to become registered by the Health Professions Council (HPC).

By means of role play and group work drama therapists help people to overcome psychological problems.

Have you had any drama therapy?

.................................................................................................

.................................................................................................

If so was it helpful or not and why?

.................................................................................................

.................................................................................................

If you have not had this type of therapy would you be interested in trying it?

.................................................................................................

.................................................................................................

# PSYCHODRAMA

Psychodrama is a form of drama therapy which was developed by Jacob Moreno in 1932 and explores emotions and relationships that trouble you through role play. Within this therapy the group acts out scenes from a member of the group's past to work through difficult emotions. Psychodrama can be fun and helps you to gain confidence in your relationships.

Psychodramatists are generally psychotherapists who have gone on to specialise in this creative type of therapy and are accredited by the United Kingdom Council for Psychotherapy as British Psychodrama Association (BPA).

Sessions usually last from one to two hours and are usually part of group therapy, but can also be used in individual therapy.

Have you had any psychodrama therapy?

.............................................................................................

.............................................................................................

If so was it helpful or not and why?

.............................................................................................

.............................................................................................

If you have not had this type of therapy would you be interested in trying it?

.............................................................................................

.............................................................................................

Talking to others with similar experiences has also been known to be beneficial to some sufferers.

# SUPPORT GROUPS

Support groups are groups of people with similar experiences who come together on a regular basis to discuss problems and share experiences, with the aim of helping each other through their distress.

You might choose to speak to close friends or family regarding how you are feeling, but there might be times when you would prefer to talk things through with someone you don't know and support groups could be one way of achieving this.

Support groups offer:

- companionship with others with similar problems as yourself
- support and understanding of your situation
- information about treatments
- recommendations of medical professions
- support from others on ways of coping with the challenges you are confronted with due to your condition.

Have you attended any support groups?

........................................................................................

........................................................................................

If so was it helpful or not and why?

........................................................................................

........................................................................................

If you have not attended any support groups which ones might you be interested in?

........................................................................................

........................................................................................

At the end of the workbook there are contact addresses and numbers for support groups.

## ▶ WHAT ARE THE ROLES OF PROFESSIONALS WHO TREAT ME?

The differences between the role of the psychiatrist and psychologist and their qualifications can sometimes be confusing. Below are short descriptions of psychiatrists, psychologists and mental health nurses.

### PSYCHIATRIST

What is your understanding of the role and training of a psychiatrist?

........................................................................................

........................................................................................

........................................................................................

Psychiatrists are medically trained doctors who look after patients with mental health problems and who are qualified to prescribe medication.

A psychiatrist first trains for five years to obtain their medical degree, then after medical school, they work as a trainee for two years on a foundation programme in a hospital to further their knowledge and skills and then they complete a further six years of speciality within psychiatry. Specialities include:

■ General adult psychiatry
■ old age psychiatry
■ child and adolescent psychiatry
■ psychotherapy
■ forensic psychiatry
■ learning disability.

The Royal College of Psychiatrists is the professional and educational organisation for psychiatrists.

## PSYCHOLOGIST

What is your understanding of the role and training of a psychologist?

. . . . . . . . . . . . . . . . . . . . . . . . . . . . . . . . . . . . . . . . . . . . . . . . . . . . . . . . . . . . . . . . . . . . . . . . . . . . . .

. . . . . . . . . . . . . . . . . . . . . . . . . . . . . . . . . . . . . . . . . . . . . . . . . . . . . . . . . . . . . . . . . . . . . . . . . . . . . .

. . . . . . . . . . . . . . . . . . . . . . . . . . . . . . . . . . . . . . . . . . . . . . . . . . . . . . . . . . . . . . . . . . . . . . . . . . . . . .

Psychology is the study of the mind and behaviour and psychologists provide a talking therapy which helps those with difficulties to overcome and understand their problems. They are unable to prescribe medication.

A psychologist first trains for three years to obtain their degree in psychology and then undertakes a further three years' training to qualify as a chartered psychologist. These further specialised subjects include:

- clinical psychologist
- counselling psychologist
- educational psychologist
- forensic psychologist
- health psychologist
- neuropsychologist
- occupational psychologist
- sports and exercise psychologist
- teacher and researchers in psychology

The British Psychological Society is the professional organisation for psychologists and runs a Directory of Chartered Psychologists which lists those psychologists who have had their qualifications and training accepted as being of sufficient standard. The website for this is at the end of the workbook.

## MENTAL HEALTH NURSES

What is your understanding of the role and training of a mental health nurse?

. . . . . . . . . . . . . . . . . . . . . . . . . . . . . . . . . . . . . . . . . . . . . . . . . . . . . . . . . . . . . . . . . . . . . . . . . . . . . .

. . . . . . . . . . . . . . . . . . . . . . . . . . . . . . . . . . . . . . . . . . . . . . . . . . . . . . . . . . . . . . . . . . . . . . . . . . . . . .

. . . . . . . . . . . . . . . . . . . . . . . . . . . . . . . . . . . . . . . . . . . . . . . . . . . . . . . . . . . . . . . . . . . . . . . . . . . . . .

Mental Health Nurses care for people with mental illness or mental distress and can work in hospitals and the community supporting those with mental health issues.

A mental health nurse first trains for three years to obtain their degree or diploma specialising in the mental health branch of nursing. Nurses can then further their career by studying for a degree in specific areas of mental health nursing and therapies.

The Nursing and Midwifery Council is the professional organisation for nurses and midwives.

## ▶ WHAT DIFFICULTIES MIGHT I ANTICIPATE REGARDING A WORKING RELATIONSHIP WITH MY THERAPIST?

Due to the in-depth work you will be exploring with your therapist, they may become an important figure in your life. This in itself may cause you problems due to how you see yourself within relationships with others.

Strong feelings that may come within therapy may be:

- You may develop a strong attachment with your therapist causing you to feel strongly dependent on them.
- This strong attachment may at times cause you to experience feelings of abandonment and rejection during sessions.
- Due to your 'black and white thinking' or 'splitting' there may be times when you are extremely angry and hate the therapist and other times when you think they are the best ever therapist you have ever had.
- Your fear of abandonment and rejection may trigger your defence mechanisms (coping responses to protect you from stressful or threatening situations) by rejecting the therapist before they reject you and finishing the therapy before any real work is done.

The above emotions are explained in more detail in Session 6.

Have you ever experienced any of the above feelings when working with a therapist?

.................................................................................................

.................................................................................................

.................................................................................................

A good therapist would be aware of the above struggles you have within a relationship and work with you on how to cope and manage your difficult emotions. If you really want therapy to work and are completely honest with yourself and your therapist your treatment is more likely to be successful.

If you feel that talking therapies is the next step for you approach your GP and he will refer you to one of the talking therapies which are available free on the NHS either at your GP's surgery, at a hospital, or from a local community mental health team.

Qualified professionals in the NHS who provide talking therapies are:

- psychologists
- psychiatrists
- counsellors

- psychotherapists
- social workers
- mental health nurses.

There may be a long waiting list, but on 10 October 2007 Health Secretary Alan Johnson announced a £170 million funding to be spent on talking treatments. He stated that this funding will be spread over three to four years, with £30 million being available next year, and GPs will be able to refer patients within the next few years (News BBC, 2007).

Don't let the thought of a waiting list put you off as it is possible that you may not have a waiting list in your area and if you do you have made a very important step in helping yourself to recover.

Your GP can also refer you to a local voluntary organisation or you can approach them yourself, for example, Mind.

You can contact agencies outside the NHS for therapists who work privately, but it can be expensive. First check with the United Kingdom Council for Psychotherapy and the British Association for Counselling and Psychotherapy before you commence private therapy regarding their credibility. Contact details are at the end of session.

The Department of Health's booklet 'Choosing Talking Therapies' will give you valuable information regarding this type of therapy and again contact details are at the end of workbook.

There are other physical therapies e.g. massage, reflexology, relaxation and yoga which can be used alongside talking therapies.

Would you be interested in the above physical therapies?

. . . . . . . . . . . . . . . . . . . . . . . . . . . . . . . . . . . . . . . . . . . . . . . . . . . . . . . . . . . . . . . . . . . . . . . . . . . . . . . . . . . .

. . . . . . . . . . . . . . . . . . . . . . . . . . . . . . . . . . . . . . . . . . . . . . . . . . . . . . . . . . . . . . . . . . . . . . . . . . . . . . . . . . . .

Taking therapies cannot be speeded up and must be allowed to take its course, so it is important that you gather as much support as you can during this difficult time.

It is not going to be easy uncovering these distressing emotions which you have buried for so long, but part of the process of healing involves identifying and feeling them however difficult that might seem to you. Because you are not used to your feelings you may feel overwhelmed when they are released from deep within you, but remember however hard it seems now it will be all worth it in the end.

If you have decided to progress with talking therapies be strong and remember you are not alone in your suffering as there are many other sufferers of Borderline Personality Disorder who are going through the same thing. There are professionals who can help you so make use of their knowledge and support and let them help you to be the person you really want to be and no longer controlled by your symptoms.

If you need more time to consider talking therapies that is OK as well, but use the time to research and join support groups which have a good understanding of your disorder so that you can build up a plan on how to move forward.

▶ **End-of-session Questionnaire**

What three important things have you learnt and will take away with you from Session 4 (you may need to browse through the session again to jog your memory).

1........................................................................................

..........................................................................................

..........................................................................................

..........................................................................................

..........................................................................................

..........................................................................................

..........................................................................................

..........................................................................................

..........................................................................................

..........................................................................................

..........................................................................................

2........................................................................................

..........................................................................................

..........................................................................................

..........................................................................................

..........................................................................................

..........................................................................................

..........................................................................................

..........................................................................................

..........................................................................................

..........................................................................................

3........................................................................................

..........................................................................................

..........................................................................................

..........................................................................................

..........................................................................................

..........................................................................................

..........................................................................................

..........................................................................................

..........................................................................................

# Session 5

> ### Questionnaire

These questions are not meant to be seen as a test. They are only a means of sharing information and getting you to think about your condition before you start your session. If you are not sure make a guess; there are no right or wrong answers.

What medication are you currently taking?

Do you have any unhelpful side effects from your medication?

# Session 5

During this session we will be looking at the most commonly asked questions regarding Borderline Personality Disorder.

1. How can medication help with the symptoms of Borderline Personality Disorder?

2. How can you work with your GP regarding your prescribed medication?

3. What is the most commonly prescribed medication?

# Session 5

## ▶ HOW CAN MEDICATION HELP WITH THE SYMPTOMS OF BORDERLINE PERSONALITY DISORDER?

Medication prescribed by a psychiatrist or GP can be useful when working alongside 'talking therapies' as it has been seen that the combination of psychotherapy and medication appears to provide the best results for the treatment of sufferers with Borderline Personality Disorder. American Psychiatric Association (2001).

There are no specific drugs are actually licensed to treat Borderline Personality Disorder, but medicines are often prescribed to sufferers to help cope with specific symptoms, for example:

■ reducing your symptoms of depression
■ improving your impulse control
■ helping to reduce your stress
■ stabilising your mood
■ helping with your paranoia thoughts
■ reducing your anxiety
■ reducing your angry behaviour

What medication have you been prescribed that has been helpful in treating certain symptoms of your condition?

...................................................................................................

...................................................................................................

...................................................................................................

If the symptoms of your condition can be improved, 'talking therapy' would have a better chance of working.

When you visit your GP or psychiatrist it would be helpful if you could develop a good working relationship with them with regard to your prescribed medication. This would increase your chances of recovery.

What experiences have you had with your GP or psychiatrist regarding taking your prescribed medication?

...................................................................................................

...................................................................................................

...................................................................................................

...................................................................................................

## ▶ HOW CAN YOU WORK WITH YOUR GP REGARDING YOUR PRESCRIBED MEDICATION?

Together you and your GP or psychiatrist can work on the following four steps which will build up a trusting relationship for you both:

### STEP ONE

*Look at the symptoms of your Borderline Personality Disorder and together with your doctor explore the options of which medication would benefit you the most.*

What symptoms of your condition do you think medication may help with?

. . . . . . . . . . . . . . . . . . . . . . . . . . . . . . . . . . . . . . . . . . . . . . . . . . . . . . . . . . . . . . . . . . . . . . . . . . . . . . . . . . . . . . . .

. . . . . . . . . . . . . . . . . . . . . . . . . . . . . . . . . . . . . . . . . . . . . . . . . . . . . . . . . . . . . . . . . . . . . . . . . . . . . . . . . . . . . . . .

. . . . . . . . . . . . . . . . . . . . . . . . . . . . . . . . . . . . . . . . . . . . . . . . . . . . . . . . . . . . . . . . . . . . . . . . . . . . . . . . . . . . . . . .

### STEP TWO

*When you have made a decision on which medication you want to take, agree on a length of time for which you will take them.*

How would you weigh up the pros and cons of your prescribed medication?

. . . . . . . . . . . . . . . . . . . . . . . . . . . . . . . . . . . . . . . . . . . . . . . . . . . . . . . . . . . . . . . . . . . . . . . . . . . . . . . . . . . . . . . .

. . . . . . . . . . . . . . . . . . . . . . . . . . . . . . . . . . . . . . . . . . . . . . . . . . . . . . . . . . . . . . . . . . . . . . . . . . . . . . . . . . . . . . . .

. . . . . . . . . . . . . . . . . . . . . . . . . . . . . . . . . . . . . . . . . . . . . . . . . . . . . . . . . . . . . . . . . . . . . . . . . . . . . . . . . . . . . . . .

### STEP THREE

*Don't stop taking the medication without talking to your doctor first (some medications should not be stopped suddenly). Meet with your doctor to review the prescribed medication and discuss any side effects if you have any.*

If you stopped taking your medication in the past, what were the reasons?

. . . . . . . . . . . . . . . . . . . . . . . . . . . . . . . . . . . . . . . . . . . . . . . . . . . . . . . . . . . . . . . . . . . . . . . . . . . . . . . . . . . . . . . .

. . . . . . . . . . . . . . . . . . . . . . . . . . . . . . . . . . . . . . . . . . . . . . . . . . . . . . . . . . . . . . . . . . . . . . . . . . . . . . . . . . . . . . . .

. . . . . . . . . . . . . . . . . . . . . . . . . . . . . . . . . . . . . . . . . . . . . . . . . . . . . . . . . . . . . . . . . . . . . . . . . . . . . . . . . . . . . . . .

### STEP FOUR

*If there is no improvement after an identified length of time ask your GP or psychiatrist if you could stop the medication and discuss other options.*

How do you feel about going through the above steps with your GP or psychiatrist?

.............................................................................

.............................................................................

.............................................................................

## ▶ WHAT IS THE MOST COMMONLY PRESCRIBED MEDICATION?

Below is some basic information about medication to treat Borderline Personality Disorder. For more detailed information about prescribed medication you will find helpful website details at the end of the workbook. You must also speak to your doctor or mental health professional for more information regarding your prescribed medication.

The most commonly prescribed medicines for Borderline Personality Disorder

American Psychiatric Association (2001) and Soloff PH (2000) are:

- antidepressants
- antipsychotic
- mood stabilisers.

These will be discussed below:

### ANTIDEPRESSANTS

Do you know how antidepressants work?

.............................................................................

.............................................................................

.............................................................................

Your brain is made up of many different cells but the main type is called a neurone. We are born with millions of these neurones and they have the ability to gather and transmit electrochemical signals or messages – just like the circuits in a computer.

Scientists have learnt a lot about these neurones or nerve cells, by studying the synapse. A synapse is a small gap that separates one nerve cell from another. This is the place where information gets passed from one nerve cell to the next nerve cell with the help of special chemicals called neurotransmitters.

If there are too many or too few of these neurotransmitters, you may develop headaches, depression, or other mental health problems. Two of these neurotransmitters or chemical messengers are called serotonin and noradrenaline and when they are released from nerve cells in the brain they lighten your mood.

Skodol *et al.* (2002) stated that sufferers of Borderline Personality Disorder have been shown to have a disturbance of the neurotransmitter serotonin. One group of antidepressants is called SSRIs (Selective Serotonin Reuptake Inhibitors) which increase the serotonin activity in the brain.

Some SSRIs which balance the serotonin levels in the brain and are used to treat Borderline Personality Disorder include:

■ Sertraline
■ Fluoxetine
■ Paroxetine
■ Citalopram
■ Fluvoxamine

Have you been prescribed any SSRI medication and if so what dosage?

..............................................................................................................
..............................................................................................................
..............................................................................................................

Another type of antidepressant is called SNRI (Serotonin and Noradrenaline Reuptake Inhibitors) and they increase both serotonin and noradrenaline activity in the brain.

Some SNRIs which balance the serotonin and noradrenaline levels in the brain and are used to treat Borderline Personality Disorder include:

■ Venlafaxine
■ Duloxetine

Have you been prescribed any SNRI medication and if so what dosage?

..............................................................................................................
..............................................................................................................
..............................................................................................................

**Side effects of antidepressant medication**

Medicines and their possible side effects can affect individual people in different ways; the following are some of the side effects that are known to be linked with both SSRIs and SNRIs. Because a side effect is mentioned below, it does not mean that all people using this medicine will experience it.

■ nausea
■ dry mouth
■ loss of appetite
■ diarrhoea
■ weight gain or weight loss
■ anxiety or irritability
■ problems sleeping or drowsiness
■ loss of sexual desire or ability
■ headaches
■ dizziness
■ vivid dreams at night.

Try not to be worried about the above list as you may get some mild side effects or you may not get any. These side effects generally wear off over a couple of weeks as your body gets used to the medication. It is a good idea for you to have a list of side effects so that you can notice them if they happen.

It is important that you do not suddenly stop taking your antidepressant medication (especially SSRIs) as this could cause you unpleasant side effects. Speak to your doctor if you are not finding them helpful.

Have you experienced any side effects whilst taking antidepressants?

.................................................................................................................

.................................................................................................................

.................................................................................................................

It can take up to two to four weeks for you to notice any real difference to your mood, but it is very important that you continue taking your medication; but if you have any distressing thoughts or feelings or are concerned about some side effects in any way, you must speak to your doctor.

The British National Formulary (BNF, 2006) states that you must never abruptly stop taking antidepressants, but the dosage should be reduced gradually under the supervision of a doctor. If you suddenly stopped your medication it could cause you to experience some unpleasant side effects or cause you to have a relapse in your symptoms of Borderline Personality Disorder. Also be aware that this medication may reduce your ability to drive or operate machinery safely; also avoid alcohol whilst taking antidepressants.

Finding the right antidepressant and dosage that works for you is very important, but you will need to work with your doctor on this.

## ANTIPSYCHOTIC

Antipsychotic medication works by balancing the levels of a different neurotransmitter in the brain and this chemical messenger is called dopamine. Some antipsychotic medication works both on dopamine and serotonin levels.

However, at low doses, these medications are often used to treat anxiety, distorted thinking, e.g. paranoia, anger and self harm behaviour, which is associated with Borderline Personality Disorder. American Psychiatric Association (2001).

Antipsychotic medication is divided into two types: typical and atypical.

Typical (conventional) antipsychotics are the older type of medication that is currently available and was first developed in the 1950s; the following typical antipsychotic medications that have been helpful in treating Borderline Personality Disorder are:

- Haloperidol
- Flupenthixol
- Chlorpromazine
- Trifluoperazine.

Have you been prescribed typical antipsychotic medication and if so what dosage?

....................................................................................................

....................................................................................................

....................................................................................................

Atypical (newer) antipsychotic medication has mostly been developed since the early 1990s: the following typical antipsychotic medications that have been helpful in treating Borderline Personality Disorder are:

- Olanzapine
- Quetiapine
- Aripiprazole
- Risperidone
- Clozapine.

Have you been prescribed atypical antipsychotic medication and if so what dosage?

....................................................................................................

....................................................................................................

....................................................................................................

**Side effects of antipsychotic medication**

- stiffness
- dry mouth
- shaking and trembling
- constipation
- drowsiness
- sun sensitivity
- blurred vision
- hypersalavation or too much saliva
- amenorrhoea (absence of periods)
- sexual dysfunction
- weight gain

Try not to be worried about the above list as you may get some mild side effects or you may not get any. These side effects generally wear off over a couple of weeks as your body gets used to the medication. It is a good idea for you to have a list of side effects so that you can notice them if they happen.

Have you experienced any side effects whilst taking antipsychotic medication?

....................................................................................................

....................................................................................................

....................................................................................................

Tardive dyskinesia is a rare side effect of antipsychotic medication and is the development of uncontrollable movements, usually of the face, lips and tongue. It occurs in about 20 per cent of sufferers who are on larger doses of typical antipsychotic medication.

If you have any distressing thoughts or feelings or are concerned about some side effects in any way, you must speak to your doctor.

If you have been prescribed Clozapine you need to be monitored very carefully because Clozapine medication can cause a problem with your white blood cells whereby your white blood cell count becomes low and it would be hard for you to fight infections. Regular blood tests would carefully monitor your white cell count and if it falls too low, you might have to stop taking Clozapine.

## MOOD STABILISERS

Not all sufferers with Borderline Personality Disorder are helped by antipsychotic or antidepressant medication. In this situation mood stabilisers have been shown to help reduce symptoms, they can either be used alongside antipsychotic and antidepressant medication or used on their own and are prescribed to regulate emotions and mood swings. Sufferers with mood swings also find that some anti-epileptic drugs are useful.

Mood stabilisers that have been found to be helpful in treating Borderline Personality Disorder are:

- Carbamazepine
- Valproate
- Lithium.

Have you been prescribed mood stabilising medication and if so what dosage?

..................................................................................................

..................................................................................................

..................................................................................................

### Carbamazepine

Carbamazepine is an anti epileptic medication which is also prescribed as a mood stabiliser.

*Side effects of carbamazepine include:*

- dry mouth and throat
- constipation
- unsteadiness
- drowsiness
- loss of appetite
- nausea
- vomiting.

Try not to be worried about the above list as you may get some mild side effects or you may not get any. These side effects generally wear off over a couple of weeks as your body gets used to the medication. It is a good idea for you to have a list of side effects so that you can notice them if they happen.

Sufferers who are prescribed Carbamazepine need to have blood tests to monitor their liver function and blood cell count.

If you have any distressing thoughts or feelings or are concerned about some side effects in any way, you must speak to your doctor.

Have you been prescribed Carbamazepine and if so what dosage?

. . . . . . . . . . . . . . . . . . . . . . . . . . . . . . . . . . . . . . . . . . . . . . . . . . . . . . . . . . . . . . . . . . . . . . . . . . . . . . . . . . . . . . . . . . . .

. . . . . . . . . . . . . . . . . . . . . . . . . . . . . . . . . . . . . . . . . . . . . . . . . . . . . . . . . . . . . . . . . . . . . . . . . . . . . . . . . . . . . . . . . . . .

**Valproate**

Semisodium Valproate or Depakote helps to treat sufferers with mood swings by increasing the actions of neurotransmitters or chemical messengers (Gamma Amino Butyric Acid) GABA in the brain.

*Side effects of Valproate medication include:*

- nausea
- vomiting
- diarrhoea
- increase in appetite
- blurred vision
- dizziness.

Try not to be worried about the above list as you may get some mild side effects or you may even not get any. These side effects generally wear off over a couple of weeks as your body gets used to the medication. It is a good idea for you to have a list of side effects so that you can notice them if they happen.

If you have any distressing thoughts or feelings or are concerned about some side effects in any way, you must speak to your doctor.

Have you been prescribed Valproate and if so how what dosage?

. . . . . . . . . . . . . . . . . . . . . . . . . . . . . . . . . . . . . . . . . . . . . . . . . . . . . . . . . . . . . . . . . . . . . . . . . . . . . . . . . . . . . . . . . . . .

. . . . . . . . . . . . . . . . . . . . . . . . . . . . . . . . . . . . . . . . . . . . . . . . . . . . . . . . . . . . . . . . . . . . . . . . . . . . . . . . . . . . . . . . . . . .

## LITHIUM

Lithium is used to treat mood swings although little is known how lithium works. Because lithium is similar to the sodium in salt it is important to have regular blood tests to measure the amount of lithium in your blood and also thyroid function, kidney function and blood cell count.

*Some of the side effects of lithium medication are:*

- fine tremor of hands
- nausea
- vomiting
- diarrhoea
- metallic taste in mouth
- feeling thirsty
- passing lot of urine.

Try not to be worried about the above list as you may get some mild side effects or you may not get any. These side effects generally wear off over a couple of weeks as your body gets used to the medication. It is a good idea for you to have a list of side effects so that you can notice them if they happen.

If you experience blurred vision, drowsiness, muscle weakness, giddiness with abnormal muscle movements, severe tremor and increased gastric disturbances you must contact your doctor.

Also contact your doctor if you have any distressing thoughts or feelings and are concerned about some side effects in any way.

Have you been prescribed lithium if so what dose (liquid or tablet)?

. . . . . . . . . . . . . . . . . . . . . . . . . . . . . . . . . . . . . . . . . . . . . . . . . . . . . . . . . . . . . . . . . . . . . . . . . . . . . . . . . . . . . . . . . . . . . . . . . . . . . .

. . . . . . . . . . . . . . . . . . . . . . . . . . . . . . . . . . . . . . . . . . . . . . . . . . . . . . . . . . . . . . . . . . . . . . . . . . . . . . . . . . . . . . . . . . . . . . . . . . . . . .

As already mentioned, if you feel unwell or if you have concerns about any side effects mentioned in this session you will need to seek advice. If you feel ill call your doctor straight away. For more advice you could also call NHS Direct on 0845 46 47.

It would be advisable for female sufferers to seek advice from their GP or psychiatrist regarding their medication if they are planning to start a family or are breastfeeding.

There is no medication that will cure Borderline Personality Disorder but the aim of prescribed medication is to help you cope with any distressing symptoms especially whilst you are working with your therapist during talking treatment. As you make progress towards your recovery you will need less medication.

## ▶ End-of-session Questionnaire

What three important things have you learnt and will take away with you from Session 5 (you may need to browse through the session again to jog your memory).

1. . . . . . . . . . . . . . . . . . . . . . . . . . . . . . . . . . . . . . . . . . . . . . . . . . . . . . . . . . . . . . . . . . . . . . . . . . . . . . . . .
. . . . . . . . . . . . . . . . . . . . . . . . . . . . . . . . . . . . . . . . . . . . . . . . . . . . . . . . . . . . . . . . . . . . . . . . . . . . . . . . . . . .
. . . . . . . . . . . . . . . . . . . . . . . . . . . . . . . . . . . . . . . . . . . . . . . . . . . . . . . . . . . . . . . . . . . . . . . . . . . . . . . . . . . .
. . . . . . . . . . . . . . . . . . . . . . . . . . . . . . . . . . . . . . . . . . . . . . . . . . . . . . . . . . . . . . . . . . . . . . . . . . . . . . . . . . . .
. . . . . . . . . . . . . . . . . . . . . . . . . . . . . . . . . . . . . . . . . . . . . . . . . . . . . . . . . . . . . . . . . . . . . . . . . . . . . . . . . . . .
. . . . . . . . . . . . . . . . . . . . . . . . . . . . . . . . . . . . . . . . . . . . . . . . . . . . . . . . . . . . . . . . . . . . . . . . . . . . . . . . . . . .
. . . . . . . . . . . . . . . . . . . . . . . . . . . . . . . . . . . . . . . . . . . . . . . . . . . . . . . . . . . . . . . . . . . . . . . . . . . . . . . . . . . .
. . . . . . . . . . . . . . . . . . . . . . . . . . . . . . . . . . . . . . . . . . . . . . . . . . . . . . . . . . . . . . . . . . . . . . . . . . . . . . . . . . . .
. . . . . . . . . . . . . . . . . . . . . . . . . . . . . . . . . . . . . . . . . . . . . . . . . . . . . . . . . . . . . . . . . . . . . . . . . . . . . . . . . . . .
. . . . . . . . . . . . . . . . . . . . . . . . . . . . . . . . . . . . . . . . . . . . . . . . . . . . . . . . . . . . . . . . . . . . . . . . . . . . . . . . . . . .

2. . . . . . . . . . . . . . . . . . . . . . . . . . . . . . . . . . . . . . . . . . . . . . . . . . . . . . . . . . . . . . . . . . . . . . . . . . . . . . . . .
. . . . . . . . . . . . . . . . . . . . . . . . . . . . . . . . . . . . . . . . . . . . . . . . . . . . . . . . . . . . . . . . . . . . . . . . . . . . . . . . . . . .
. . . . . . . . . . . . . . . . . . . . . . . . . . . . . . . . . . . . . . . . . . . . . . . . . . . . . . . . . . . . . . . . . . . . . . . . . . . . . . . . . . . .
. . . . . . . . . . . . . . . . . . . . . . . . . . . . . . . . . . . . . . . . . . . . . . . . . . . . . . . . . . . . . . . . . . . . . . . . . . . . . . . . . . . .
. . . . . . . . . . . . . . . . . . . . . . . . . . . . . . . . . . . . . . . . . . . . . . . . . . . . . . . . . . . . . . . . . . . . . . . . . . . . . . . . . . . .
. . . . . . . . . . . . . . . . . . . . . . . . . . . . . . . . . . . . . . . . . . . . . . . . . . . . . . . . . . . . . . . . . . . . . . . . . . . . . . . . . . . .
. . . . . . . . . . . . . . . . . . . . . . . . . . . . . . . . . . . . . . . . . . . . . . . . . . . . . . . . . . . . . . . . . . . . . . . . . . . . . . . . . . . .
. . . . . . . . . . . . . . . . . . . . . . . . . . . . . . . . . . . . . . . . . . . . . . . . . . . . . . . . . . . . . . . . . . . . . . . . . . . . . . . . . . . .

3. . . . . . . . . . . . . . . . . . . . . . . . . . . . . . . . . . . . . . . . . . . . . . . . . . . . . . . . . . . . . . . . . . . . . . . . . . . . . . . . .
. . . . . . . . . . . . . . . . . . . . . . . . . . . . . . . . . . . . . . . . . . . . . . . . . . . . . . . . . . . . . . . . . . . . . . . . . . . . . . . . . . . .
. . . . . . . . . . . . . . . . . . . . . . . . . . . . . . . . . . . . . . . . . . . . . . . . . . . . . . . . . . . . . . . . . . . . . . . . . . . . . . . . . . . .
. . . . . . . . . . . . . . . . . . . . . . . . . . . . . . . . . . . . . . . . . . . . . . . . . . . . . . . . . . . . . . . . . . . . . . . . . . . . . . . . . . . .
. . . . . . . . . . . . . . . . . . . . . . . . . . . . . . . . . . . . . . . . . . . . . . . . . . . . . . . . . . . . . . . . . . . . . . . . . . . . . . . . . . . .
. . . . . . . . . . . . . . . . . . . . . . . . . . . . . . . . . . . . . . . . . . . . . . . . . . . . . . . . . . . . . . . . . . . . . . . . . . . . . . . . . . . .
. . . . . . . . . . . . . . . . . . . . . . . . . . . . . . . . . . . . . . . . . . . . . . . . . . . . . . . . . . . . . . . . . . . . . . . . . . . . . . . . . . . .
. . . . . . . . . . . . . . . . . . . . . . . . . . . . . . . . . . . . . . . . . . . . . . . . . . . . . . . . . . . . . . . . . . . . . . . . . . . . . . . . . . . .
. . . . . . . . . . . . . . . . . . . . . . . . . . . . . . . . . . . . . . . . . . . . . . . . . . . . . . . . . . . . . . . . . . . . . . . . . . . . . . . . . . . .

# Session 6

▶ **Questionnaire**

These questions are not meant to be seen as a test. They are only a means of sharing information and getting you to think about your condition before you start your session. If you are not sure make a guess; there are no right or wrong answers.

1. What sort of things do you like to do when you have time to yourself?

2. What are your dreams and wishes for the future?

# Session 6

During this session we will be looking at a 'Wheel of Borderline Personality Disorder' where certain areas of your life are affected by your disorder.

1. Wheel of mood swings

2. Wheel of psychosis

3. Wheel of impulsive behaviours

4. Wheel of emptiness and boredom

5. Wheel of suicidal ideas

6. Wheel of abandonment

7. Wheel of relationships

8. Wheel of self harming

9. Wheel of anger

10. Wheel of self identity

# Session 6

Mahari (1999) described suffering from Borderline Personality Disorder as being much like a hamster in a cage using loads of energy walking non-stop on a wheel and getting nowhere, just going round and round in circles. This hamster wheel starts when you have a problem; you don't know how to sort it out, then you blame yourself and mentally beat yourself up and then, because of this constant churning that is going on in your head, things seem to get worse and the wheel keeps spinning.

Have you felt like this at times?

.........................................................................................

.........................................................................................

.........................................................................................

Mahari stated that for you to begin to journey towards oneself is to step off the wheel and begin to find the door to the cage. This may be a really scary thought for you, but if you are fed up of running on the wheel then Session 6 and support from your health worker will be a start to helping and guiding you through.

Some self help coping strategies are suggested throughout this session, however, they are not to be seen as a form of treatment, but as a way working through difficult emotions whilst you are engaged in talking treatment (Session 4) and medication (Session 5). Explore, with your therapist, some of these suggestions and whether they would be helpful to your particular needs. This session cannot replace the valuable role a therapist has with regard to supporting and guiding you along your road to recovery.

Below we will be looking at a 'wheel of life' where each segment represents a symptom of your Borderline Personality Disorder. Consider each segment, rating each one from 0–10 with 10 being the most difficult symptom for you to cope with at present. This will highlight areas of your life where you may be using a lot of negative energy and where it seems that you are not getting anywhere, much like the hamster in the cage. If you are putting too much negative energy into one or more areas you will not have enough energy to focus your attention on an alternative segment which may have a more positive outcome to help you find the door to your cage.

---

**If one area is out of balance it will affect all others.**

---

# WHEEL OF A BORDERLINE PERSONALITY DISORDER LIFE

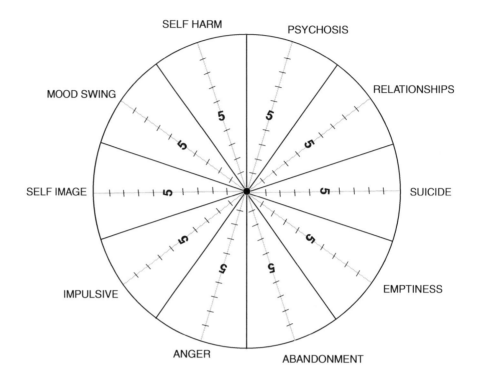

In this session we will be looking at some useful ideas on how to control and cope with some of your symptoms.

Before we continue have you rated the above wheel from 0–10 and identified the symptoms which you have difficulties with and would like things to be different?

.............................................................................................

.............................................................................................

.............................................................................................

.............................................................................................

Do you want to have an understanding of the issues that trouble you?

.............................................................................................

Because you have Borderline Personality Disorder it does not mean you can never live a normal life like those people who do not suffer from the same disorder; you can also have a successful life, but it means you will have to learn how to understand parts of yourself.

Some of you may not be ready to see this disorder as a challenge and may want to be seen as a 'victim' of your diagnosis and want others to rally around you. If this is the stage that you are at, then that really is fine. Nearly all illnesses, physical or psychological, make us feel like this at some stage, making us think:

■ 'what's the point?'

- 'nothing will change'
- 'it sounds like hard work and I don't have the energy'.

But eventually there will be a time where you want something different and you will want to live your life with more passion and hope.

How uncomfortable do you feel when thinking about this challenge?

. . . . . . . . . . . . . . . . . . . . . . . . . . . . . . . . . . . . . . . . . . . . . . . . . . . . . . . . . . . . . . . . . . . . . . . . .

If you are feeling uncomfortable thinking about this challenge this is quite normal, but if you want to step off the hamster's wheel and do something different you need to take a risk.

As already mentioned you are not responsible for what happened to you in your past, but you are responsible for your actions and the choices you make thereafter.

Your life from there on has always been your responsibility and you can choose to free yourself, but that will only be when you make decisions with the help of health professionals.

Are you ready to take up the challenge?

. . . . . . . . . . . . . . . . . . . . . . . . . . . . . . . . . . . . . . . . . . . . . . . . . . . . . . . . . . . . . . . . . . . . . . . . .

Now you have highlighted the areas into which you put your most negative energy, you need to complete the next 'wheel of life' which will instead focus on what positive energy you can focus on if you really want to. Actively working on improving any part of your life will give you a sense of achievement and help you develop a more positive mental attitude.

You will probably not have problems with symptoms in all the segments of the wheel, but we will be looking at each segment in a bit more detail.

## ▶ MOOD SWINGS

Mood swings are a symptom of your inner distress, but the following session is not meant as a form of treatment, but an exploration of coping strategies to work alongside talking therapies. Hopefully, this session will help you to understand why you are the way you are so that you can seek further help through talking therapy.

If you have difficulty coping with your moods how do you think your life would look if you had a little more control over your moods?

. . . . . . . . . . . . . . . . . . . . . . . . . . . . . . . . . . . . . . . . . . . . . . . . . . . . . . . . . . . . . . . . . . . . . . . . .

. . . . . . . . . . . . . . . . . . . . . . . . . . . . . . . . . . . . . . . . . . . . . . . . . . . . . . . . . . . . . . . . . . . . . . . . .

What would be important to you in this?

. . . . . . . . . . . . . . . . . . . . . . . . . . . . . . . . . . . . . . . . . . . . . . . . . . . . . . . . . . . . . . . . . . . . . . . . .

. . . . . . . . . . . . . . . . . . . . . . . . . . . . . . . . . . . . . . . . . . . . . . . . . . . . . . . . . . . . . . . . . . . . . . . . .

Nothing will happen unless we create a chance for it to come about.

It might be helpful for you to browse through Session 3 again on page 29 to recap on mood swings.

Below we will be looking at a 'wheel of mood swings' where each segment represents skills you can learn to help control your moods. Consider each segment, rating each one from 0–10 with 10 being the most difficult skill to manage.

## WHEEL OF MOOD SWINGS

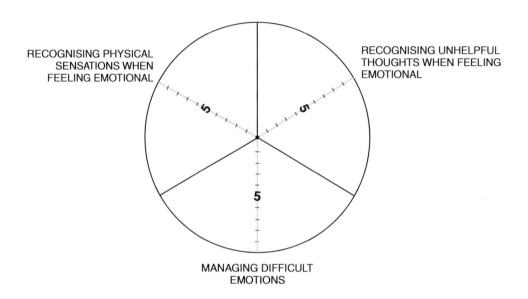

RECOGNISING PHYSICAL SENSATIONS WHEN FEELING EMOTIONAL

RECOGNISING UNHELPFUL THOUGHTS WHEN FEELING EMOTIONAL

MANAGING DIFFICULT EMOTIONS

Think of a situation when you last felt emotional in your mood: .

When . . . . . . . . . . . . . . . . . . . . . . . . . . . . . . . . . . . . . . . . . . . . . . . . . . . . . . . . . . . . . . . . . . . . . . . . . . . . . . . . . . . . . . . . .

Where . . . . . . . . . . . . . . . . . . . . . . . . . . . . . . . . . . . . . . . . . . . . . . . . . . . . . . . . . . . . . . . . . . . . . . . . . . . . . . . . . . . . . . .

What happened . . . . . . . . . . . . . . . . . . . . . . . . . . . . . . . . . . . . . . . . . . . . . . . . . . . . . . . . . . . . . . . . . . . . . . . . . . . . .

Our emotions can quickly change from feeling really good to feeling pretty miserable in a matter of minutes. Those who suffer from Borderline Personality Disorder undergo mood shifts more drastically than others, experiencing feelings, for example, anxiousness and anger, more intensely.

Your mood might feel to you at times to be out of control, but whether you are aware of it or not, you do, up to a point, have some control over what you do with your feelings.

### RECOGNISING PHYSICAL SENSATIONS WHEN FEELING EMOTIONAL

Are you aware when your mood changes? Did you experience any physical sensations that may indicate to you that all is not as it should be?

- racing heart and palpitations
- stomach ache
- sweating

- tense muscles – e.g. shoulders, neck, back and head
- feeling faint and dizzy
- shallow breathing – breathlessness, fast breathing
- redness in face
- eyes seem blurred
- dry mouth
- feeling nauseous
- shaking
- headache

List below your physical sensations:

. . . . . . . . . . . . . . . . . . . . . . . . . . . . . . . . . . . . . . . . . . . . . . . . . . . . . . . . . . . . . . . . . . . . . . . . . . . . . . . . . . . . .

. . . . . . . . . . . . . . . . . . . . . . . . . . . . . . . . . . . . . . . . . . . . . . . . . . . . . . . . . . . . . . . . . . . . . . . . . . . . . . . . . . . . .

. . . . . . . . . . . . . . . . . . . . . . . . . . . . . . . . . . . . . . . . . . . . . . . . . . . . . . . . . . . . . . . . . . . . . . . . . . . . . . . . . . . . .

If you recognise these as warning signs that you are becoming emotional this is the first step to gaining control over your emotions. Once you have noticed your body's indicators that you are becoming emotional you need to take heed before your behaviour escalates causing you to behave in a way that you might later regret.

You can think of it as a red traffic light – **STOP**

| |
|---|
| It would be helpful for you to say to yourself: <br><br> **When I experience** . . . . . . . . . . . . . . . . . . . . . . . . . . . . . . . . . . . . . . . . . . . . . . . . . . . . . . . . . . . . . <br><br> . . . . . . . . . . . . . . . . . . . . . . . . . . . . . . . . . . . . . . . . . . . . . . . . . . . . . . . . . . . . . . . . . . . . . . <br><br> 'I will stop and think for a moment about where this is going to lead me'. |

When you begin to feel ill at ease with yourself or your nerves start to get on edge you can comfort yourself emotionally by focusing your attention on your five senses: hearing, sight, smell, taste and touch. This will take you away from any troubled thoughts and feelings.

*Say to yourself:*

At this moment I can hear:

. . . . . . . . . . . . . . . . . . . . . . . . . . . . . . . . . . . . . . . . . . . . . . . . . . . . . . . . . . . . . . . . . . . . . . . . . . . . . . . . . . . . .

. . . . . . . . . . . . . . . . . . . . . . . . . . . . . . . . . . . . . . . . . . . . . . . . . . . . . . . . . . . . . . . . . . . . . . . . . . . . . . . . . . . . .

At this moment I can see:

. . . . . . . . . . . . . . . . . . . . . . . . . . . . . . . . . . . . . . . . . . . . . . . . . . . . . . . . . . . . . . . . . . . . . . . . . . . . . . . . . . . . .

. . . . . . . . . . . . . . . . . . . . . . . . . . . . . . . . . . . . . . . . . . . . . . . . . . . . . . . . . . . . . . . . . . . . . . . . . . . . . . . . . . . . .

At this moment I can smell:

．．．．．．．．．．．．．．．．．．．．．．．．．．．．．．．．．．．．．．．．．．．．．．．．．．．．．．．．．．．．．．．．．．．．．．．．．．．．．．．．．．．．

．．．．．．．．．．．．．．．．．．．．．．．．．．．．．．．．．．．．．．．．．．．．．．．．．．．．．．．．．．．．．．．．．．．．．．．．．．．．．．．．．．．．

At this moment I can taste:

．．．．．．．．．．．．．．．．．．．．．．．．．．．．．．．．．．．．．．．．．．．．．．．．．．．．．．．．．．．．．．．．．．．．．．．．．．．．．．．．．．．．

．．．．．．．．．．．．．．．．．．．．．．．．．．．．．．．．．．．．．．．．．．．．．．．．．．．．．．．．．．．．．．．．．．．．．．．．．．．．．．．．．．．．

At this moment I can feel:

．．．．．．．．．．．．．．．．．．．．．．．．．．．．．．．．．．．．．．．．．．．．．．．．．．．．．．．．．．．．．．．．．．．．．．．．．．．．．．．．．．．．

．．．．．．．．．．．．．．．．．．．．．．．．．．．．．．．．．．．．．．．．．．．．．．．．．．．．．．．．．．．．．．．．．．．．．．．．．．．．．．．．．．．．

Below is an activity you could complete with your mental health worker which highlights how focusing on your five senses helps you comfort yourself and gives you some breathing space to consider what you are going to do next with these difficult feelings.

You will need your favourite sweet before you can carry on with the next part of this session.

Firstly, pick up your sweet and look at it in detail and say out loud, if you wish, the colours, the size, the texture and also what is written on the wrapper.

．．．．．．．．．．．．．．．．．．．．．．．．．．．．．．．．．．．．．．．．．．．．．．．．．．．．．．．．．．．．．．．．．．．．．．．．．．．．．．．．．．．．

．．．．．．．．．．．．．．．．．．．．．．．．．．．．．．．．．．．．．．．．．．．．．．．．．．．．．．．．．．．．．．．．．．．．．．．．．．．．．．．．．．．．

Next, open the wrapper and describe what it smells like.

．．．．．．．．．．．．．．．．．．．．．．．．．．．．．．．．．．．．．．．．．．．．．．．．．．．．．．．．．．．．．．．．．．．．．．．．．．．．．．．．．．．．

Raise the sweet to your mouth and notice which muscles in your hand you use.

．．．．．．．．．．．．．．．．．．．．．．．．．．．．．．．．．．．．．．．．．．．．．．．．．．．．．．．．．．．．．．．．．．．．．．．．．．．．．．．．．．．．

Touch the sweet with your tongue before taking a bite, what do you notice about the flavour?

．．．．．．．．．．．．．．．．．．．．．．．．．．．．．．．．．．．．．．．．．．．．．．．．．．．．．．．．．．．．．．．．．．．．．．．．．．．．．．．．．．．．

Take a bite and notice your teeth cutting through the sweet, what muscles are used in your face when your jaw moves up and down?

．．．．．．．．．．．．．．．．．．．．．．．．．．．．．．．．．．．．．．．．．．．．．．．．．．．．．．．．．．．．．．．．．．．．．．．．．．．．．．．．．．．．

Can you feel the saliva in your mouth?

．．．．．．．．．．．．．．．．．．．．．．．．．．．．．．．．．．．．．．．．．．．．．．．．．．．．．．．．．．．．．．．．．．．．．．．．．．．．．．．．．．．．

Chew it slowly, and see how long it is before you need to swallow?

．．．．．．．．．．．．．．．．．．．．．．．．．．．．．．．．．．．．．．．．．．．．．．．．．．．．．．．．．．．．．．．．．．．．．．．．．．．．．．．．．．．．

Do this with every bite until you are finished.

Describe your feelings regarding this exercise:

. . . . . . . . . . . . . . . . . . . . . . . . . . . . . . . . . . . . . . . . . . . . . . . . . . . . . . . . . . . . . . . . . . . . . . . . . . . . . . . . . . . . . . . . . . . .

. . . . . . . . . . . . . . . . . . . . . . . . . . . . . . . . . . . . . . . . . . . . . . . . . . . . . . . . . . . . . . . . . . . . . . . . . . . . . . . . . . . . . . . . . . . .

. . . . . . . . . . . . . . . . . . . . . . . . . . . . . . . . . . . . . . . . . . . . . . . . . . . . . . . . . . . . . . . . . . . . . . . . . . . . . . . . . . . . . . . . . . . .

Below are other ideas that might help you to stimulate your five senses.

### HEARING

- Listen to soothing classical music.
- Walk along the seafront and listen to the waves.
- Walk in the park and listen to the rustling of leaves under your feet.
- Listen to birds singing in the garden.
- Hum a tune or sing along to a record.
- Listen to yourself breathing.
- Listen to some invigorating music, like rock.

### SMELL

- Put on your favourite perfume.
- Polish your furniture and smell the air.
- Smell some potpourri in your home.
- Bake a cake or bread.
- Smell the flowers in a flower shop.
- Light a scented candle.
- Smell newly cut grass.

### TASTE

- Taste your favourite meal or drink.
- Treat yourself to an ice cream.
- Suck a mint.

**TOUCH**

- Have a soothing bath
- Stroke a cat/dog.
- Have a massage.
- Put moisturising lotion on body.
- Sit in really comfortable chair.
- Soak feet in bowl of water or at the seaside.
- Hug someone.

**VISION**

- Find a picture which has some meaning to you and look at it.
- At night time look at the stars.
- Sit in a park and watch what is going on around you.
- Look at some art in a book.
- Sit in a castle or other historic monument or church.
- Look for a bright item of clothing that you could buy.
- Light a candle and look at the flicker of the flame.
- Buy a bunch of your favourite flowers.
- Watch a funny film.

Try some of these mentioned ideas with the help of your psychologist or mental health worker, to find which technique works best for you

Marsha Linehan (1993) stated that you need to be 'comforting, nurturing, gentle and kind to oneself' and one way of doing this is to soothe each of the five senses you have.

### RECOGNISING UNHELPFUL THOUGHTS WHEN FEELING EMOTIONAL

Stop and think for a moment about the last time you felt upset. What came first, was it a thought or a feeling?

. . . . . . . . . . . . . . . . . . . . . . . . . . . . . . . . . . . . . . . . . . . . . . . . . . . . . . . . . . . . . . . . . . . . . . . . . . . . . . . . . . . . .

Would you be surprised if you were told that it is actually a thought that comes before a feeling? For example, you might hear a noise in the middle of the night and think 'it's a burglar' and then feel scared.

But if you thought the noise was your cat you would not feel scared.

Can you think of other examples whereby you experienced a thought which was followed by a feeling?

. . . . . . . . . . . . . . . . . . . . . . . . . . . . . . . . . . . . . . . . . . . . . . . . . . . . . . . . . . . . . . . . . . . . . . . . . . . . . . . . . . . . .

. . . . . . . . . . . . . . . . . . . . . . . . . . . . . . . . . . . . . . . . . . . . . . . . . . . . . . . . . . . . . . . . . . . . . . . . . . . . . . . . . . . . .

Do you sometimes get caught up in unhelpful thoughts which have caused you great distress?

. . . . . . . . . . . . . . . . . . . . . . . . . . . . . . . . . . . . . . . . . . . . . . . . . . . . . . . . . . . . . . . . . . . . . . . . . . . . . . . . . . . . .

If you are a person who constantly thinks about the past or who worries about the future you have become a prisoner of your own thoughts.

You may need to be reminded that the past has gone and cannot be changed and the future is not here yet and you cannot predict it. But what takes place between the past and the future is this present moment which is the here and now.

As already mentioned, our thoughts have a powerful effect on how we feel which will without doubt shape our mood. The most common thinking errors for those who suffer from Borderline Personality Disorder are catastrophic and dichotomous.

When you catastrophise this means that you exaggerate the consequences if things go wrong and assume that things will be disastrous and these thoughts will cause a negative change to your mood.

What catastrophic thoughts have you experienced which caused your mood to change for the worst?

. . . . . . . . . . . . . . . . . . . . . . . . . . . . . . . . . . . . . . . . . . . . . . . . . . . . . . . . . . . . . . . . . . . . . . . . . . . . . . . . . . . . .

. . . . . . . . . . . . . . . . . . . . . . . . . . . . . . . . . . . . . . . . . . . . . . . . . . . . . . . . . . . . . . . . . . . . . . . . . . . . . . . . . . . . .

Did your worst fear come true?

. . . . . . . . . . . . . . . . . . . . . . . . . . . . . . . . . . . . . . . . . . . . . . . . . . . . . . . . . . . . . . . . . . . . . . . . . . . . . . . . . . . . .

When you have dichotomous thoughts it means that you are thinking in black and white terms. This means someone or something is either good or bad with no in betweens. For example, if you are not beautiful you must be ugly or if something is wrong then it is completely rubbish.

What dichotomous thoughts have you experienced which have caused your mood to change for the worst?

. . . . . . . . . . . . . . . . . . . . . . . . . . . . . . . . . . . . . . . . . . . . . . . . . . . . . . . . . . . . . . . . . . . . . . . . . . . . . . . . . . . . .

. . . . . . . . . . . . . . . . . . . . . . . . . . . . . . . . . . . . . . . . . . . . . . . . . . . . . . . . . . . . . . . . . . . . . . . . . . . . . . . . . . . . .

If you experience any of the above thinking errors speak to your psychologist.

If you experience a change in your mood remind yourself of the times when you have coped under difficult circumstances.

In the past I have dealt with:

...............................................................................................

...............................................................................................

...............................................................................................

...............................................................................................

And I have some good qualities:

...............................................................................................

...............................................................................................

...............................................................................................

...............................................................................................

...............................................................................................

That won't disappear just because my mood is up and down.

## MANAGING DIFFICULT EMOTIONS

'Feelings are just that – feelings; they let us know when something isn't right. It's what we do with them that matters' (Anne Wilson Schaef, 1996).

You can learn a lot about yourself by keeping an eye on your feelings because they provide some clues about you. The best way to deal with feelings is to firstly feel them, understand why you have them by exploring them with someone you trust and then release them. When you run away from your feelings these feelings linger around and won't go away. If you are having difficulty working out your emotions, get help from a professional who will guide and support you through your most difficult emotions.

Learning to manage your feelings and calm yourself down when you are upset is one of the most important things you can do and will enable you to work towards a happier life which you surely deserve.

Marsha Lineham (1993) suggested practicing 'mindfulness' which is a core exercise that is used in dialectic behaviour therapy (DBT) and that to be mindful is to realise that 'thoughts are just thoughts' and to 'learn to be in control of your mind instead of letting your mind control you'.

Mindfulness is a 2,500-year-old concept which is borrowed from Eastern Buddhist meditation practices which helps you to focus your awareness on something else other than possible hurtful emotions. Goleman (1988) defined mindfulness as 'facing bare facts of experience, seeing each event as though occurring for the first time'.

Being aware of an experience from moment to moment without drifting into thoughts from the past or concerns about the future helps you to stay calm and gets you to focus on something else other than your distressing thoughts.

The following activity will help you to understand the concept of mindfulness. Get someone to time you and focus your attention on your breathing and nothing else for the next 30 seconds. Say to yourself things like 'I am inhaling', 'I am exhaling' and 'my mind is at peace'. Close your eyes if you want to.

Describe how you felt:

. . . . . . . . . . . . . . . . . . . . . . . . . . . . . . . . . . . . . . . . . . . . . . . . . . . . . . . . . . . . . . . . . . . . . . . . . . . . . . . . . .

Did you manage to just focus on your breathing or did your thoughts wander off to other things?

. . . . . . . . . . . . . . . . . . . . . . . . . . . . . . . . . . . . . . . . . . . . . . . . . . . . . . . . . . . . . . . . . . . . . . . . . . . . . . . . . .

If so, don't worry, after a bit of practice you will be able to master this skill.

If you were able to stay in the moment you have proved to yourself that you can focus your mind, which will help you to manage some of the stresses of everyday life and let difficult emotions pass over you.

So to recap, 'mindfulness' is about what you pay attention to and about you getting some control of where your awareness goes. You can practice mindfulness by doing other things that focus on what you are doing at the moment.

Last time you had a bath what can you remember about it?

. . . . . . . . . . . . . . . . . . . . . . . . . . . . . . . . . . . . . . . . . . . . . . . . . . . . . . . . . . . . . . . . . . . . . . . . . . . . . . . . . .

. . . . . . . . . . . . . . . . . . . . . . . . . . . . . . . . . . . . . . . . . . . . . . . . . . . . . . . . . . . . . . . . . . . . . . . . . . . . . . . . . .

---

**You could have a bath mindfully**

Feel the water on your skin, smell the bubble bath, be conscious of where every part of your body is in the bath, feel the texture of your skin while you wash with soap and a sponge, listen to the water going down the plughole.

---

Last time you did some housework what can you remember about it?

. . . . . . . . . . . . . . . . . . . . . . . . . . . . . . . . . . . . . . . . . . . . . . . . . . . . . . . . . . . . . . . . . . . . . . . . . . . . . . . . . .

. . . . . . . . . . . . . . . . . . . . . . . . . . . . . . . . . . . . . . . . . . . . . . . . . . . . . . . . . . . . . . . . . . . . . . . . . . . . . . . . . .

> **You can do your housework mindfully**
>
> Feel the vacuum cleaner in your hand and notice how heavy or light it is, smell the furniture spray and notice how shiny the furniture is, when you iron clothes smell the heat from the iron and notice the texture and colour of the clothes you iron and listen for the steam which comes out of the iron.

Last time you went for a walk what can you remember about it?

...................................................................................................

...................................................................................................

> **You can walk mindfully**
>
> Concentrate on how the ground feels beneath your feet. Is it soft, hard, wet or dry? What is your breathing like while you are walking? Look around you and describe what you see, feel the wind blowing in your hair or feel the sun on your face. Stay in the present and let all your thoughts go up into the sky and enjoy the moment.

Next time you do any of the above again, write down what you noticed:

...................................................................................................

...................................................................................................

...................................................................................................

We have thousands of thoughts that go through our heads every day and as already mentioned some thoughts are helpful and some unhelpful. If you experience unhelpful thinking whilst doing these tasks you are free to let the thoughts go and remind yourself that these thoughts may not be reliable, mindfulness allows you to declutter your thoughts and clear your mind.

Mindfulness is a skill which needs to be practiced, preferably every day and is particularly helpful when you feel like reacting to any difficult emotions you might have and it will prevent you from seeking instant relief through self harm for example. Beside mindfulness there are other suggestions that might help your mood and these include:

Get your *hands busy*

- draw a picture of yourself using brightly coloured pens
- buy a colouring book and some pencils
- make a collage and glue all different materials and use coloured pencils
- make up a story and type it out
- write a letter to friends
- write a poem
- pursue any hobbies you might have
- open a dictionary and learn a new word

- do a crossword
- learn to play solitaire card games
- play a guitar
- write your feelings in a journal
- do some finger painting with food, for example, ice cream or jam
- do a jigsaw.

Get your *mind rested:*

- have a relaxing bubble bath
- massage body lotion and oils all over your body
- curl up in bed and listen to calming music
- call a friend and chat about nothing in particular
- watch a soppy film, watch a funny film
- watch cartoons
- get yourself a warm drink and curl up on the settee with a cuddly toy
- ask someone for a cuddle
- walk in the countryside
- read a book
- stroke an animal
- sunbathe in the sun
- sit by the beach and listen to the waves
- wear something that makes you feel good
- give yourself a facial
- relax and close your eyes and breathe slowly
- treat yourself to something nice to eat
- walk a dog
- hug yourself.

Which of the suggestions above would you like to try if you experienced feeling low in your mood?

..............................................................................................

..............................................................................................

It can be hard to focus and remember good things when you are in the midst of a negative feeling. So when you are in a better mood make yourself a 'comforting tool box'. This is your own special box, for example, a shoebox that you can decorate and which contains anything that would keep you focused and give you comfort when things get too rough for you. You could include in this box:

- a CD or tape of your favourite songs
- a colouring book and pens
- photos of family or friends
- notes or letters that mean something comforting to you
- a photo of yourself which makes you feel good

- old birthday, Christmas cards etc. that hold special memories for you
- special stuffed toy
- flash card made by you of encouraging messages to yourself
- a list of phone numbers you could ring that would give you comfort
- a list of addresses you could write to people who would give you comfort
- stories you have written about any special memories you might have
- favourite perfume
- blank pieces of paper for you to draw or paint a picture on with pens and paints
- favourite DVD or video
- favourite sweet
- favourite bubble bath
- favourite magazine
- comic
- a gift someone gave to you with special meaning
- a gem stone
- a comforting prayer or a cross
- a boiled sweet.

You must only open your 'comforting tool box' in an emergency or it will not feel as special as you want it to be and you can change some of the contents every few months or add others to it.

You can start today looking for special things to put in your 'comfort tool box'. List the items you are going to put in today:

..........................................................................................................

..........................................................................................................

..........................................................................................................

On page 93 is a pleasant chart for you to fill in each day before you go to bed and it will remind you of any meaningful things that may have happened to you that day. Also, during the day you can focus on noticing things that you could perhaps add to your chart each day.

The above suggestions alone are not enough to cope with your mood swings. These ideas can be helpful if they are working alongside talking therapies and some sufferers may also need to consider medication if their symptoms are too distressing for them.

| I saw today | I thought of today |
|---|---|
| **I smelt today** | **I learnt about myself today** |
| **I tasted today** | **Someone did for me today** |
| **I heard today** | **I did something for someone today** |
| **I touched today** | **I am looking forward to** |

**Photocopy and complete this at the end of each day**

## ▶ Wheel of 'mood swings' end-of-session Questionnaire

What three important things have you learnt and will take away with you from the mood swings session (you may need to browse through the session again to jog your memory).

1.................................................................................................
.................................................................................................
.................................................................................................
.................................................................................................
.................................................................................................
.................................................................................................
.................................................................................................
.................................................................................................
.................................................................................................
.................................................................................................

2.................................................................................................
.................................................................................................
.................................................................................................
.................................................................................................
.................................................................................................
.................................................................................................
.................................................................................................
.................................................................................................
.................................................................................................

3.................................................................................................
.................................................................................................
.................................................................................................
.................................................................................................
.................................................................................................
.................................................................................................
.................................................................................................
.................................................................................................

## ▶ PSYCHOSIS

Psychosis is a symptom of your inner distress and the following session is not meant as a form of treatment, but only to give ideas of coping strategies to work alongside medication and talking therapies. Hopefully this session will help you to understand why you are the way you are so that you can seek further help through therapy.

If you have difficulties with psychosis symptoms how differently do you think your life would be if you were able to cope with these feelings more effectively?

.................................................................................

.................................................................................

What would be important to you about this?

.................................................................................

.................................................................................

Nothing will happen unless we create a chance for it to come about.

It might be helpful for you to browse through Session 3 again on page 30 to recap on the symptoms of psychosis.

Below we will be looking at a 'wheel of psychosis' where each segment represents skills you can learn in how to manage stress. Consider each segment, rating each one from 0–10 with 10 being the most difficult skill to manage with regard to your symptoms of psychosis.

## WHEEL OF PSYCHOSIS

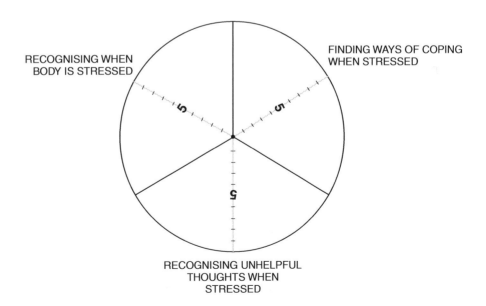

RECOGNISING WHEN
BODY IS STRESSED

FINDING WAYS OF COPING
WHEN STRESSED

RECOGNISING UNHELPFUL
THOUGHTS WHEN
STRESSED

As already mentioned in Session 3 you may sometimes experience paranoid ideation which is when you get feelings of persecution whereby you feel that others are out to harm you in some way. These feelings can last for a few minutes or up to a few hours and usually occur when you are feeling stressed and can be very distressing for you. Also you may experience dissociative symptoms which are equally distressing. This is when you feel disconnected from yourself and you feel like you are 'running on automatic'.

Marsha Lineham (1993) stated that those who have a Borderline Personality Disorder are born with a tendency to react more strongly to lower levels of stress than other people, also those who were brought up in environments where they felt devalued and not highly thought of. These people become confused when their feelings are confronted under vulnerable conditions.

Stress can be described as tension, anxiety, pressure, worry and strain and it can have an enormous impact on how you see the world around you.

Think of a situation when you last became stressed:

When . . . . . . . . . . . . . . . . . . . . . . . . . . . . . . . . . . . . . . . . . . . . . . . . . . . . . . . . . . . . . . . . . . . . . . . . . . . . . . . . . . . . . . .

Where . . . . . . . . . . . . . . . . . . . . . . . . . . . . . . . . . . . . . . . . . . . . . . . . . . . . . . . . . . . . . . . . . . . . . . . . . . . . . . . . . . . . . .

What happened . . . . . . . . . . . . . . . . . . . . . . . . . . . . . . . . . . . . . . . . . . . . . . . . . . . . . . . . . . . . . . . . . . . . . . . . . .

. . . . . . . . . . . . . . . . . . . . . . . . . . . . . . . . . . . . . . . . . . . . . . . . . . . . . . . . . . . . . . . . . . . . . . . . . . . . . . . . . . . . . . . . . . .

### RECOGNISING WHEN BODY IS STRESSED

Next explore what your trigger points are, that is what feelings or situations are more likely to make you feel stressed:

. . . . . . . . . . . . . . . . . . . . . . . . . . . . . . . . . . . . . . . . . . . . . . . . . . . . . . . . . . . . . . . . . . . . . . . . . . . . . . . . . . . . . . . . . . .

. . . . . . . . . . . . . . . . . . . . . . . . . . . . . . . . . . . . . . . . . . . . . . . . . . . . . . . . . . . . . . . . . . . . . . . . . . . . . . . . . . . . . . . . . . .

The next stage is recognising any physical sensations you might have prior to feeling stressed:

- racing heart and palpitations
- stomach ache
- sweating
- tense muscles – e.g. shoulders, neck, back and head
- feeling faint and dizzy
- shallow breathing – breathlessness, fast breathing
- redness in face
- eyes seem blurred
- dry mouth
- feeling nauseous
- shaking
- headache

List below your physical sensations:

. . . . . . . . . . . . . . . . . . . . . . . . . . . . . . . . . . . . . . . . . . . . . . . . . . . . . . . . . . . . . . . . . . . . . . . . . . . . . . . . . . . . . . . . . . .

You can recognise the above as warning signs that you may be reaching a point where your stress levels are increasing and then you may be able to do something more positive which will prevent this stress from overwhelming you and causing you to experience brief episodes of paranoid ideation or dissociation.

If you do not address the warning signs you may then experience a thought that will make your distorted ideas stronger.

If this happens then stop and think of it as a red traffic light – STOP

> It would be helpful for you to say to yourself:
>
> **When I experience** . . . . . . . . . . . . . . . . . . . . . . . . . . . . . . . . . . . . . . . . . . . . . . . . . . . . . . . . . . . . . . . . . . . . . . . . . . .
>
> . . . . . . . . . . . . . . . . . . . . . . . . . . . . . . . . . . . . . . . . . . . . . . . . . . . . . . . . . . . . . . . . . . . . . . . . . . . . . . . . . . . . . . . . . .
>
> . . . . . . . . . . . . . . . . . . . . . . . . . . . . . . . . . . . . . . . . . . . . . . . . . . . . . . . . . . . . . . . . . . . . . . . . . . . . . . . . . . . . . . . . . .
>
> 'I will stop and think for a moment where this is going to lead me'.

## RECOGNISING UNHELPFUL THOUGHTS WHEN STRESSED

Each one of us has our own level of tolerating situations and changes that life can bring along, but when circumstances become particularly difficult we describe our experience as **being under stress.**

There are all sorts of situations that can be stressful, and stress affects anyone and everyone, but is especially difficult if you suffer from borderline personality disorder. Some of the most important areas of your life for causing stress might be:

- pressure at work
- problems with family, especially arguments
- money worries, especially if you are in debt due to overspending
- relationship problems, especially feelings of rejection and abandonment
- accommodation problems
- pain due to physical problems
- problems with the law due to your anger.

For what reasons have you felt stressed in the past?

. . . . . . . . . . . . . . . . . . . . . . . . . . . . . . . . . . . . . . . . . . . . . . . . . . . . . . . . . . . . . . . . . . . . . . . . . . . . . . . . . . . . . . . . . .

. . . . . . . . . . . . . . . . . . . . . . . . . . . . . . . . . . . . . . . . . . . . . . . . . . . . . . . . . . . . . . . . . . . . . . . . . . . . . . . . . . . . . . . . . .

Our thoughts and the way we think have a very powerful effect on our feelings. Dr Albert Ellis (1962) founder of Rational Emotive Therapy identified the responsibility we each have for our thoughts, beliefs and the way we talk to ourselves when we are involved in stressful situations; he called this the ABC model.

'A' refers to an experience which will trigger off thoughts which is 'B', and in turn will produce a reaction of feelings and behaviours which is 'C'.

- ■ Something happens e.g. someone looks at you intently for a second 'A'.
- ■ The belief you have regarding the person who gave you the look is: 'they are going to harm me or they don't like me'. 'I must be a terrible person for people not to like me' 'B'.
- ■ You have an emotional reaction to this belief which is that you will give that person distance and be hypervigilant to other people's behaviour around you and this will confirm your fear that you are a terrible person 'C'.

Have you experienced something similar?

..............................................................................................................

..............................................................................................................

..............................................................................................................

Are you able to understand how the ABC model shows that 'A' (experience) does not cause 'C' (behaviour)? It is 'B' (thought) that causes 'C' (behaviour). Discuss this further with your mental health worker or psychologist.

Ellis stated that you must devise a plan to challenge these thoughts.

One way of doing this is by not trying to guess what other people are thinking, because by doing this you will be treating your suspicion like it was fact, which is not completely true. No one yet has mastered the skill to read minds although some stage entertainers claim they can.

Has someone said or done something to you which caused you some stress?

Describing the thoughts that ran through your head, are you absolutely sure you knew what they were thinking without asking them first?

..............................................................................................................

..............................................................................................................

If someone looked at you in a way that made you feel a bit uncomfortable list other reasons that they may not like you for why they are looking like that:

..............................................................................................................

..............................................................................................................

There is more than one reason why people might be looking at you other than that they think you are a terrible person. It might be that they thought they mistook you for someone else or that they looked at you because they liked the trendy jumper you were wearing. Try not to take things personally. It may be nothing at all to do with you but something to do with them.

Have you ever looked at or talked about someone to another person?

..............................................................................................................

..............................................................................................................

Was your gossip nasty or was it inoffensive. If you did not mean any harm then maybe they don't either. Put the 'look' you received into perspective and try to understand it from a different point of view.

Discuss the ABC model in more detail with your psychologist and look at the Albert Ellis website, the details of which are at the end of the workbook.

### HELPFUL COPING STRATEGIES WHEN STRESSED

Here are some more unhelpful coping strategies that you might do if you feel stressed.

- smoking
- using illicit drugs or alcohol to cope
- avoiding the problems
- taking it out on others either verbally or physically
- isolating yourself and not wanting to be around others
- denying that you have problems
- being overactive and very busy
- over-eating or under-eating
- self-harm.

Here are some helpful coping strategies to relieve stress and keep you feeling well:

- listening to music
- watching TV
- having a bath
- write your thoughts in a diary
- exercise or playing sports
- practice relaxation techniques
- problem solve by breaking the problem down into manageable parts
- enjoy a healthy diet and adequate sleep
- distraction e.g. counting to 1–10
- self praise for remaining in control
- focusing on the task on hand
- do some gardening and sit in the sun
- visit places of interest
- attend a centre
- visit friends or family
- paint or draw a picture
- give yourself a compliment
- stretch like a cat
- think of your favourite place
- relax your face and smile
- try some positive self talk – 'just relax', 'breathe', 'it may not be what I am thinking', 'Its my illness making me think like this and trying to trick me', 'I can get through his'

- ask for help
- look through your comforting box (page 91)
- practice mindfulness (page 89)
- focus on your five senses (page 85).

Which would give you a more positive outcome of a situation: the helpful or the unhelpful?

Which of the above have you usually done when you feel stressed?

...........................................................................................

...........................................................................................

...........................................................................................

...........................................................................................

...........................................................................................

...........................................................................................

When you have identified physical sensations on page 98 the following steps may be helpful to you:

**Step One**

When you have felt a bit uneasy but don't know why, or you experience any physical sensations, say this to yourself or approach someone you trust and say it to them.

Is this something you feel you could do; what is your plan for step one if you experience the above sensations?

...........................................................................................

...........................................................................................

**Step Two**

Try and trace this back to where this uncomfortable feeling originally came from, for example, maybe someone said something to you that made you feel uneasy.

Can you think of an occasion whereby an uncomfortable situation triggered a physical sensation?

...........................................................................................

...........................................................................................

**Step Three**

Tell yourself that you are going to put this uncomfortable feeling on hold until you can give yourself space to deal with it later, practice mindfulness and focusing on your five senses (pages 85 and 89).

What other activities could you do to distract yourself from this difficult feeling?

. . . . . . . . . . . . . . . . . . . . . . . . . . . . . . . . . . . . . . . . . . . . . . . . . . . . . . . . . . . . . . . . . . . . . . . . . .

. . . . . . . . . . . . . . . . . . . . . . . . . . . . . . . . . . . . . . . . . . . . . . . . . . . . . . . . . . . . . . . . . . . . . . . . . .

**Step Four**

When you think the time is right talk to someone about this feeling or if you think you can manage this feeling on your own deal with it yourself. You might learn that this is a feeling of paranoia and the process will help you to understand your fears and concerns.

**Step Five**

When you have understood this as a feeling of paranoia let it go and take care of yourself by using strategies on page 90.

**Step Six**

Complete stress diary on page 104 on a regular basis and find alternative ways of coping more effectively with stressful situations.

The above suggestions are not enough for you to cope with your paranoid ideation or dissociative experiences. These ideas can be helpful if they are working alongside talking therapies and some sufferers may also consider medication if the symptoms are too distressing for them.

Speak to your psychologist to help you through this journey.

## ▶ STRESS DIARY

Think of a time recently whereby you felt stressed and complete the stress diary below:

Time and day:

..............................................................................................................

Briefly describe what happened:

..............................................................................................................

..............................................................................................................

..............................................................................................................

Identify the emotions you felt?

..............................................................................................................

..............................................................................................................

..............................................................................................................

What thoughts went through your mind?

..............................................................................................................

..............................................................................................................

..............................................................................................................

Which coping strategies did you use to handle the stress?

..............................................................................................................

..............................................................................................................

..............................................................................................................

Did it work?

..............................................................................................................

If not, why do you think it did not work?

..............................................................................................................

..............................................................................................................

..............................................................................................................

If your coping strategies did not work, what could you have done differently?

..............................................................................................................

..............................................................................................................

..............................................................................................................

**Photocopy the above and complete every week**

What three important things have you learnt and will take away with you from the psychosis session (you may need to browse through the session again to jog your memory)?

1 ...............................................................................................

...............................................................................................

...............................................................................................

...............................................................................................

...............................................................................................

...............................................................................................

...............................................................................................

...............................................................................................

...............................................................................................

2 ...............................................................................................

...............................................................................................

...............................................................................................

...............................................................................................

...............................................................................................

...............................................................................................

...............................................................................................

...............................................................................................

3 ...............................................................................................

...............................................................................................

...............................................................................................

...............................................................................................

...............................................................................................

...............................................................................................

...............................................................................................

...............................................................................................

## ▶ IMPULSIVE BEHAVIOURS

Impulsive behaviours are a symptom of your inner distress and the following session is not meant as a form of treatment but gives ideas of coping strategies to work alongside talking therapies. Hopefully this session will help you to understand why you are the way you are so that you can seek further help through therapy.

If you have difficulties with impulsive behaviours how differently do you think your life would be if you were able to cope with these feelings more effectively?

. . . . . . . . . . . . . . . . . . . . . . . . . . . . . . . . . . . . . . . . . . . . . . . . . . . . . . . . . . . . . . . . . . . . . . . . . . . . . . . . . . . . . . . . . . . . . . . . .

. . . . . . . . . . . . . . . . . . . . . . . . . . . . . . . . . . . . . . . . . . . . . . . . . . . . . . . . . . . . . . . . . . . . . . . . . . . . . . . . . . . . . . . . . . . . . . . . .

What would be important to you about this?

. . . . . . . . . . . . . . . . . . . . . . . . . . . . . . . . . . . . . . . . . . . . . . . . . . . . . . . . . . . . . . . . . . . . . . . . . . . . . . . . . . . . . . . . . . . . . . . . .

. . . . . . . . . . . . . . . . . . . . . . . . . . . . . . . . . . . . . . . . . . . . . . . . . . . . . . . . . . . . . . . . . . . . . . . . . . . . . . . . . . . . . . . . . . . . . . . . .

Nothing will happen unless we create a chance for it to come about.

It might be helpful for you to browse through Session 3 again on page 31 to recap on the symptoms of impulsive behaviours.

Below we will be looking at a 'wheel of impulsive' where each segment represents skills you can learn in how you can manage your impulsive actions more effectively. Consider each segment, rating each one from 0–10 with 10 being the most difficult skill to manage with regard to your symptoms of impulsive behaviour.

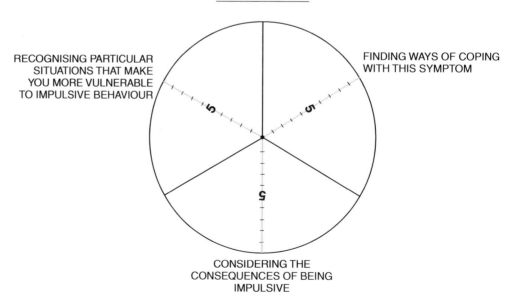

## WHEEL OF IMPULSIVE BEHAVIOUR

RECOGNISING PARTICULAR SITUATIONS THAT MAKE YOU MORE VULNERABLE TO IMPULSIVE BEHAVIOUR

FINDING WAYS OF COPING WITH THIS SYMPTOM

CONSIDERING THE CONSEQUENCES OF BEING IMPULSIVE

## RECOGNISING PARTICULAR SITUATIONS THAT MAKE YOU MORE VULNERABLE TO IMPULSIVE BEHAVIOUR

When something happens to you that causes you to experience intense emotional turmoil, do you feel compelled to react to the moment in order to escape these unbearable feelings?

There are some valid emotional reasons why you may feel a strong compulsion to:

- binge eat
- drive fast
- misuse illicit drugs
- misuse alcohol
- gamble money
- overspend
- have many casual sexual relationships.

Are you aware of the situations that make you more vulnerable to acting out your emotions with regard to the above behaviours?

.........................................................................................

.........................................................................................

.........................................................................................

Other sufferers have stated that the above behaviours have met a need in them that:

- satisfies strong tense feelings
- addresses feelings of chronic emptiness
- satisfies their struggle for control
- alters their mood state
- satisfies their feelings of boredom
- releases them from the depth of despair
- alleviates stress
- living on the edge gives them a sense of feeling alive
- escape unbearable feelings
- addresses feelings of abandonment and rejection
- forces them to do 'something' in order for them to escape from their situation
- acts as a kind of self destruction or self hate
- attempts to bring about some form of rescue from others.

Which of the above has applied to you?

.........................................................................................

.........................................................................................

.........................................................................................

Although the above impulsive behaviours are quick fixes to your difficult emotions and satisfy your emotional needs immediately, you are often left feeling much worse after the event, making you feel guilty and remorseful. You also need to identify the times when you are more vulnerable to impulsive behaviours:

1. I am vulnerable when . . . . . . . . . . . . . . . . . . . . . . . . . . . . . . . . . . . . . . . . . . . . . . . . . . . . . . . . . . . . . . . . .
2. I am vulnerable when . . . . . . . . . . . . . . . . . . . . . . . . . . . . . . . . . . . . . . . . . . . . . . . . . . . . . . . . . . . . . . . . .
3. I am vulnerable when . . . . . . . . . . . . . . . . . . . . . . . . . . . . . . . . . . . . . . . . . . . . . . . . . . . . . . . . . . . . . . . . .

## CONSIDERING THE CONSEQUENCES OF BEING IMPULSIVE

Most people are able to control their impulses and delay immediate gratification because they are aware of long-term consequences for example:

- weight gain
- unplanned pregnancies
- sexually transmitted diseases
- motor car accidents
- physical fights
- physical conditions for example liver problems
- debt collectors.

Have you suffered from some of the above consequences due to your impulsive behaviour?

. . . . . . . . . . . . . . . . . . . . . . . . . . . . . . . . . . . . . . . . . . . . . . . . . . . . . . . . . . . . . . . . . . . . . . . . . . . . . . . . . . . .

. . . . . . . . . . . . . . . . . . . . . . . . . . . . . . . . . . . . . . . . . . . . . . . . . . . . . . . . . . . . . . . . . . . . . . . . . . . . . . . . . . . .

. . . . . . . . . . . . . . . . . . . . . . . . . . . . . . . . . . . . . . . . . . . . . . . . . . . . . . . . . . . . . . . . . . . . . . . . . . . . . . . . . . . .

But because you suffer from Borderline Personality Disorder you will find it much harder to control these impulses due to feelings of anxiety or emptiness. These activities act as a distraction for you, but, unfortunately, your mistakes are repeated over and over again causing more disruption and chaos in your life.

## FINDING WAYS OF COPING WITH THIS SYMPTOM

Think of a situation when you last acted impulsively:

When . . . . . . . . . . . . . . . . . . . . . . . . . . . . . . . . . . . . . . . . . . . . . . . . . . . . . . . . . . . . . . . . . . . . . . . . . . . . .

Where . . . . . . . . . . . . . . . . . . . . . . . . . . . . . . . . . . . . . . . . . . . . . . . . . . . . . . . . . . . . . . . . . . . . . . . . . . . .

What happened . . . . . . . . . . . . . . . . . . . . . . . . . . . . . . . . . . . . . . . . . . . . . . . . . . . . . . . . . . . . . . . . . . . .

. . . . . . . . . . . . . . . . . . . . . . . . . . . . . . . . . . . . . . . . . . . . . . . . . . . . . . . . . . . . . . . . . . . . . . . . . . . . . . . . . . . .

What physical sensations did you experience prior to your impulsive behaviour?

- racing heart and palpitations
- stomach ache
- sweating
- tense muscles – e.g. shoulders, neck, back and head
- feeling faint and dizzy
- shallow breathing – breathlessness, fast breathing
- redness in face
- eyes seem blurred
- dry mouth
- feeling nausea
- shaking
- headache.

List any of the above symptoms that you experience:

................................................................................

................................................................................

What emotions did you feel during this difficult time?

................................................................................

................................................................................

What thoughts were running through your head when you were experiencing the above physical symptoms?

................................................................................

................................................................................

You can recognise the above as warning signs that you may be reaching the point where you will be feeling overwhelmed with fear and feeling vulnerable.

If this happens again then stop and think of it as a red traffic light – STOP

---

It would be helpful to say to yourself:

**When I experience**................................................................

................................................................................

................................................................................

'I will stop and think for a moment where this is going to lead me'.

---

When you have identified the above warning signs as feelings of emptiness and anxiety the following steps may be helpful to you:

**Step One**

When you have felt a bit uneasy but don't know why, or you experience any physical sensations, tell yourself this is how you feel or approach someone you trust and tell them.

Is this something you feel you could do; what is your plan for Step One if you experience any of the above sensations or feelings?

...................................................................................................

...................................................................................................

**Step Two**

Try and trace this back to where this uncomfortable feeling originally came from, for example, maybe someone said something to you that made you feel uneasy.

Can you think of any occasion whereby an uncomfortable feeling triggered a physical sensation, feeling or thought?

...................................................................................................

...................................................................................................

**Step Three**

Tell yourself that you are going to put this uncomfortable feeling on hold until you can give yourself space to deal with it later. Don't dwell on your uncomfortable feeling, but practice mindfulness and focusing on your five senses (pages 85 and 89).

What activities could you do to distract yourself from this difficult feeling?

...................................................................................................

...................................................................................................

**Step Four**

When you think the time is right, talk to someone about this feeling or if you think you can manage this feeling on your own deal with it yourself. You could reflect on the consequences of your destructive actions which might be a feeling of emptiness and anxiety, and the process will help you to understand your fears and concerns.

**Step Five**

When you have understood your feeling of emptiness and anxiety and learn to take care of yourself by using strategies on page 90.

**Step Six**

Complete stress diary on page 103 on a regular basis and find alternative ways of coping more effectively with stressful situations.

When you have identified physical, thought and emotional sensations on page 101 the following steps may be helpful to you:

- Value yourself more and you will be less likely to put yourself through any further anguish than you have already experienced.
- Recognise the patterns of your impulsive behaviour.
- Talk about your underlying emotions to others who you trust.
- Remove yourself from situations where you are more likely to be impulsive.

The above suggestions alone are not enough for you to cope with your impulsive behaviour; these ideas can be helpful if they are working alongside talking therapies with the support from your psychologist to help you through this journey.

## ► Wheel of 'impulsive behaviour' end-of-session Questionnaire

What three important things have you learnt and will take away with you from this session (you may need to browse through the session again to jog your memory).

1......................................................................................................................

..........................................................................................................................

..........................................................................................................................

..........................................................................................................................

..........................................................................................................................

..........................................................................................................................

..........................................................................................................................

..........................................................................................................................

..........................................................................................................................

..........................................................................................................................

2......................................................................................................................

..........................................................................................................................

..........................................................................................................................

..........................................................................................................................

..........................................................................................................................

..........................................................................................................................

..........................................................................................................................

..........................................................................................................................

..........................................................................................................................

3......................................................................................................................

..........................................................................................................................

..........................................................................................................................

..........................................................................................................................

..........................................................................................................................

..........................................................................................................................

..........................................................................................................................

..........................................................................................................................

..........................................................................................................................

## ► EMPTINESS AND BOREDOM

Emptiness and boredom are symptoms of your inner distress and the following session is not meant as a form of treatment, but gives ideas for coping strategies to work alongside talking therapies. Hopefully this session will help you to understand why you are the way you are so that you can seek further help through talking therapy.

If you have difficulties with feelings of emptiness and boredom how differently do you think your life would be if you were able to cope with these feelings more effectively?

. . . . . . . . . . . . . . . . . . . . . . . . . . . . . . . . . . . . . . . . . . . . . . . . . . . . . . . . . . . . . . . . . . . . . . . . . . . . . . .

. . . . . . . . . . . . . . . . . . . . . . . . . . . . . . . . . . . . . . . . . . . . . . . . . . . . . . . . . . . . . . . . . . . . . . . . . . . . . . .

. . . . . . . . . . . . . . . . . . . . . . . . . . . . . . . . . . . . . . . . . . . . . . . . . . . . . . . . . . . . . . . . . . . . . . . . . . . . . . .

What would be important to you about this?

. . . . . . . . . . . . . . . . . . . . . . . . . . . . . . . . . . . . . . . . . . . . . . . . . . . . . . . . . . . . . . . . . . . . . . . . . . . . . . .

. . . . . . . . . . . . . . . . . . . . . . . . . . . . . . . . . . . . . . . . . . . . . . . . . . . . . . . . . . . . . . . . . . . . . . . . . . . . . . .

Nothing will happen unless we create a chance for it to come about.

It might be helpful for you to browse through Session 3 again on page 32 to recap on the symptoms of emptiness and boredom.

Below we will be looking at a 'wheel of emptiness and boredom' where each segment represents skills you can learn in relation to how you can deal with these feelings more effectively. Consider each segment, rating each one from 0–10 with 10 being the most difficult skill to manage with regard to your symptoms of emptiness and boredom.

### WHEEL OF EMPTINESS AND BOREDOM

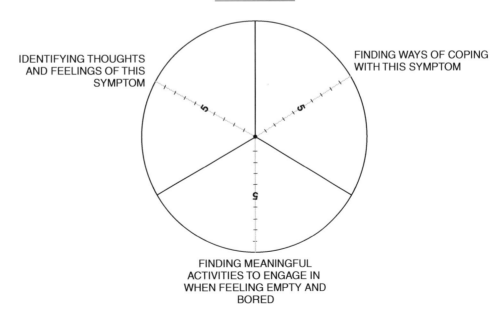

IDENTIFYING THOUGHTS AND FEELINGS OF THIS SYMPTOM

FINDING WAYS OF COPING WITH THIS SYMPTOM

FINDING MEANINGFUL ACTIVITIES TO ENGAGE IN WHEN FEELING EMPTY AND BORED

## FINDING MEANINGFUL ACTIVITIES TO ENGAGE IN WHEN FEELING EMPTY AND BORED

Some sufferers describe emptiness as a big hole in the middle of their soul and not knowing how to fill this empty space; that their feelings and emotions are not within easy reach and they can only describe an extreme vulnerability within themselves.

Would you say that you feel a kind of numbness inside or that you can't see a purpose to your life?

...................................................................................................

...................................................................................................

...................................................................................................

This might be because:

■ you lack a sense of who you are
■ you don't have any confidence in yourself
■ you don't feel good enough.

But being in this place causes you to feel a painful loneliness.

## IDENTIFYING THE THOUGHTS AND FEELINGS OF THIS SYMPTOM

Can you think of the last time that you felt empty inside?:

**When** ..............................................................................................

**Where** .............................................................................................

**What happened** .................................................................................

...................................................................................................

You may not be aware of it, but there might be situations when your feelings of isolation and emptiness could be triggered, for example, when you are around:

■ certain family members
■ situations that are new to you
■ large groups of people
■ certain people you work with.

All these could make a difference to how you feel and think about yourself and your surroundings.

Are you aware of any of the above triggers that might have caused you to feel empty inside?

...................................................................................................

...................................................................................................

Can you remember what physical sensations you experienced prior to you feeling empty?

- racing heart and palpitations
- stomach ache
- sweating
- tense muscles – e.g. shoulders, neck, back and head
- feeling faint and dizzy
- shallow breathing – breathlessness, fast breathing
- redness in face
- eyes seem blurred
- dry mouth
- feeling nausea
- shaking
- headache.

List any of above physical symptoms that you have experienced:

...................................................................................

What emotions did you feel during this difficult time?

...................................................................................

...................................................................................

What thoughts were running through your head when you were experiencing the above physical symptoms?

...................................................................................

...................................................................................

You can recognise the above as warning signs that you may be reaching the point where you might feel overwhelmed with numbness and feeling vulnerable. A need to fill this emptiness can lead you to self damaging impulses to make you feel real.

If this happens again then stop and think of it as a red traffic light – STOP

---

It would be helpful to say to yourself:

**When I experience** ...................................................

...................................................................................

...................................................................................

'I will stop and think for a moment where this is going to lead me'.

---

## FINDING WAYS OF COPING WITH THIS SYMPTOM

When you have identified the above warning signs as feelings of emptiness and boredom the following steps may be helpful to you:

When you have identified physical sensations on page 117 the following steps may be helpful to you:

**Step One**

When you have felt a bit uneasy but don't know why, or if you experience physical sensations, tell yourself that you are or approach someone you trust and tell them.

Is this something you feel you could do; what is your plan for Step One if you experience any of the above sensations?

. . . . . . . . . . . . . . . . . . . . . . . . . . . . . . . . . . . . . . . . . . . . . . . . . . . . . . . . . . . . . . . . . . . . . . . . . .

. . . . . . . . . . . . . . . . . . . . . . . . . . . . . . . . . . . . . . . . . . . . . . . . . . . . . . . . . . . . . . . . . . . . . . . . . .

**Step Two**

Try and trace this back to where this uncomfortable feeling originally came from, for example, maybe someone said something to you that made you feel uneasy.

Can you think of an occasion when an uncomfortable feeling triggered a physical sensation?

. . . . . . . . . . . . . . . . . . . . . . . . . . . . . . . . . . . . . . . . . . . . . . . . . . . . . . . . . . . . . . . . . . . . . . . . . .

. . . . . . . . . . . . . . . . . . . . . . . . . . . . . . . . . . . . . . . . . . . . . . . . . . . . . . . . . . . . . . . . . . . . . . . . . .

**Step Three**

Tell yourself that you are going to put this uncomfortable feeling on hold until you can give yourself space to deal with it, practice mindfulness and focusing on your five senses (pages 85 and 89).

What other activities could you do to distract yourself from this difficult feeling?

. . . . . . . . . . . . . . . . . . . . . . . . . . . . . . . . . . . . . . . . . . . . . . . . . . . . . . . . . . . . . . . . . . . . . . . . . .

. . . . . . . . . . . . . . . . . . . . . . . . . . . . . . . . . . . . . . . . . . . . . . . . . . . . . . . . . . . . . . . . . . . . . . . . . .

**Step Four**

When you think the time is right talk to someone about this feeling or if you think you can manage this feeling on your own, deal with it yourself. You might learn that this is a feeling of emptiness and boredom and the process will help you to understand your fears and concerns.

**Step Five**

When you have understood this feeling of emptiness let it go and take care of yourself by using strategies on page 90 and 91. Speak to your psychologist to help you through this journey.

There are also activities that you could do to find some meaning in your life which will be discussed next.

## FINDING MEANINGFUL ACTIVITIES WHEN FEELING EMPTY AND BORED

It has been said that volunteering your help and assistance to others will help to give you a sense of identity of 'who you are' and will also bring you some social contact which will ease your sense of loneliness.

Activities that may help you to manage feelings of emptiness and boredom are:

- Volunteer your time to work in charity shops.
- Volunteer your time to work in a horse sanctuary.
- Volunteer your time to work in a nursing home.
- Join a walking/rambling group.
- Volunteer your time to work with charity organisations.
- Help a friend or member of family in need.
- Do something nice for a friend or member of family e.g. bake cake.
- Join a college and learn something that interests you.

What would you like to do you which would give you some meaning to your life?

..............................................................................................................

..............................................................................................................

..............................................................................................................

..............................................................................................................

Also, owning a pet has been known to ease the feelings of emptiness in those who struggle with this emotion. Other sufferers have also been known to have felt supported by their spiritual faith.

List all the things that you have achieved (no matter how small):

..............................................................................................................

..............................................................................................................

..............................................................................................................

Set some small goals you would like for yourself for the future:

..............................................................................................................

..............................................................................................................

..............................................................................................................

..............................................................................................................

**Remember to tell yourself that you certainly do exist and you certainly deserve a meaningful life**

The above discussions alone are not enough for you to cope with your feelings of emptiness, but are suggestions to help you understand your symptoms and when working alongside talking therapies.

## ▶ Wheel of emptiness and boredom end-of-session Questionnaire

What three important things have you learnt and will take away with you from this session (you may need to browse through the session again to jog your memory).

1. ...................................................................................................................
...................................................................................................................
...................................................................................................................
...................................................................................................................
...................................................................................................................
...................................................................................................................
...................................................................................................................
...................................................................................................................
...................................................................................................................
...................................................................................................................

2. ...................................................................................................................
...................................................................................................................
...................................................................................................................
...................................................................................................................
...................................................................................................................
...................................................................................................................
...................................................................................................................
...................................................................................................................
...................................................................................................................

3. ...................................................................................................................
...................................................................................................................
...................................................................................................................
...................................................................................................................
...................................................................................................................
...................................................................................................................
...................................................................................................................
...................................................................................................................
...................................................................................................................

## ▶ SUICIDAL IDEAS

Suicidal ideation is a symptom of your inner distress but the following session is not meant as a form of treatment but gives ideas of coping strategies to work alongside talking therapies. Hopefully this session will help you to understand why you are the way you are so that you can seek further help through talking therapy.

If you have difficulties with suicidal thoughts how different do you think your life would be if you were able to cope with these distressing feelings more effectively?

.................................................................................................................................................

.................................................................................................................................................

.................................................................................................................................................

What would be important to you about this?

.................................................................................................................................................

.................................................................................................................................................

Nothing will happen unless we create a chance for it to come about.

Below we will be looking at a 'wheel of suicidal ideas' where each segment represents skills you can learn in relation to your suicidal ideation. Consider each segment, rating each one from 0–10 with 10 being the most difficult skill to manage.

## WHEEL OF SUICIDAL IDEAS

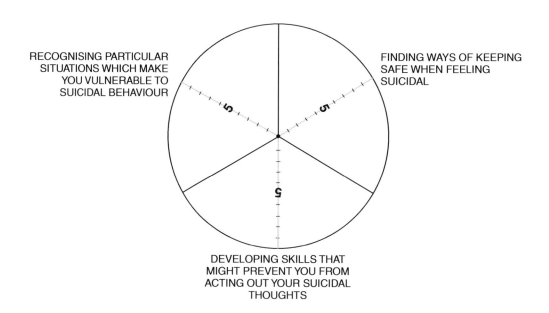

RECOGNISING PARTICULAR SITUATIONS WHICH MAKE YOU VULNERABLE TO SUICIDAL BEHAVIOUR

FINDING WAYS OF KEEPING SAFE WHEN FEELING SUICIDAL

DEVELOPING SKILLS THAT MIGHT PREVENT YOU FROM ACTING OUT YOUR SUICIDAL THOUGHTS

## RECOGNISING PARTICULAR SITUATIONS WHICH MAKE YOU MORE VULNERABLE TO SUICIDAL BEHAVIOUR?

There may have been times whereby the intense emotional pain you sometimes go through has been so bad that you have felt like ending it all. But having thoughts of ending it all does not necessarily mean that you actually want to die, but you may see it as a way out of the unbearable suffering you are experiencing at that time.

This does not mean you are terrible or a weak person, it means that you had more pain than you could cope with at that time.

Some suicide attempts may be triggered by feelings of:

- hopelessness
- intense emotional suffering
- anger
- abandonment
- frustration
- emptiness
- impulsive thoughts.

If you have had thoughts of suicide in the past what feelings triggered this notion?

. . . . . . . . . . . . . . . . . . . . . . . . . . . . . . . . . . . . . . . . . . . . . . . . . . . . . . . . . . . . . . . . . . . . . . . . . . . . . . . . .

. . . . . . . . . . . . . . . . . . . . . . . . . . . . . . . . . . . . . . . . . . . . . . . . . . . . . . . . . . . . . . . . . . . . . . . . . . . . . . . . .

. . . . . . . . . . . . . . . . . . . . . . . . . . . . . . . . . . . . . . . . . . . . . . . . . . . . . . . . . . . . . . . . . . . . . . . . . . . . . . . . .

If you suffer from the following symptoms talk to your GP as you may be suffering from depression:

- changes in sleep patterns
- changes in appetite or weight
- feelings of hopelessness
- loss of interest in the things you usually enjoyed
- loss of energy
- suicidal thoughts
- think negatively about yourself
- overwhelming feelings of guilt.

The road to recovery can be long and takes both strength and courage to get through it, but it can be achieved with support and understanding.

## DEVELOPING SKILLS THAT MIGHT PREVENT YOU FROM ACTING OUT YOUR SUICIDAL THOUGHTS

If you have had feelings of wanting to end it all you will have already found out that you can get through these strong emotional feelings. This will hopefully give you a sense of hope and remind you that you have been to the edge and managed somehow to get through it.

If you have not experienced these feelings it may give you hope that if you ever experience these feelings you are not alone in your suffering and others have managed to get through this difficult time in their lives.

Give yourself some distance between your thoughts and your actions, but this can be difficult if it seems that what ever you do it does not help or is not enough to stop the flood of painful emotions forcing it way through your whole body.

Your suicidal thoughts do not have to become a reality; don't impulsively act on your thoughts, but wait a while as there may be a part of you that wants to die, but there may also be a part of you that wants to live.

List some of the strategies that you have used in the past to cope with suicidal thoughts:

......................................................................................................

......................................................................................................

......................................................................................................

Some ways to cope with suicidal thoughts and feelings:

■ Talk to someone every day even though you might not want to.

■ Remove any items from your home that you might use to harm yourself until you feel better in your mood.

■ Avoid alcohol or illicit drugs.

■ Eat a balanced diet even if it is only in small portions.

■ If you can't sleep at night get up for a short while and watch TV or read until you are tired so that you are not lying in bed ruminating over things in your head.

■ Make a written timetable for yourself every day and do at least two 30-minute activities that give you pleasure e.g. listening to music, having a warm bath, going for a walk etc. Tick them off as you do them.

■ Browse through your 'comfort tool box' (see page 91).

■ Practice mindfulness (page 87).

■ Write yourself some self affirmation statements (helpful things to say to yourself) about why you should not kill yourself and read them when you feel troubled e.g. 'I will feel better eventually', 'Each time I cope with my fears and despair it will make me stronger', 'My life has some meaning even though I don't think so at this moment' and 'I have just got to get through a second at a time'.

Is there anything from the above list you could do to get through suicidal thoughts?

......................................................................................................

......................................................................................................

What self affirmation statements could you say to yourself?

......................................................................................................

......................................................................................................

......................................................................................................

# FINDING WAYS OF KEEPING SAFE WHEN FEELING SUICIDAL

If your suicidal thoughts become stronger or you feel the urge to act out these distressing thoughts you need to seek help straight away. Call a member of your family or a friend to go with you to your GP or accident and emergency. When you feel overwhelmed with suicidal urges you might feel that you want to be somewhere where you would feel safe and where there are people to prevent you from acting out these urges. This might mean going into hospital.

Have you been admitted to hospital because of distressing thoughts of suicide, if so what was your experience?

..........................................................................................

..........................................................................................

..........................................................................................

Unfortunately, some people have had negative experiences whilst visiting accident and emergency departments, but the NHS has new guidelines (NICE, 2006) so that you will receive the best possible care.

The community also provide crisis teams that work with sufferers and their families and your GP or mental health team will be able to refer you.

If professionals feel that you present a danger to yourself or others they may recommend that you be referred as an 'informal' or a voluntary patient for hospital assessment or treatment.

Has this ever happened to you?

..........................................................................................

..........................................................................................

You may refuse treatment when you really need it. To protect you from acting out your urges, due to your distressed state of mind, you may be compulsorily admitted or 'sectioned' under the Mental Health Act 1983 against your will. This is only used when you need an assessment or treatment and you refuse to accept it.

If has happened to you how did you feel at the time?

..........................................................................................

..........................................................................................

If you are kept in hospital, under this law you can appeal against the decision. You will be told this when you are admitted into hospital.

If you have been sectioned or detained in hospital you may be subject to a supervised discharge, this means your care will be supervised after you leave hospital. (Mind.org.uk, 2003)

A close relative has the legal right to request a mental health assessment from an approved social worker (ASW) to look at the best treatment for you, and one of those decisions may be whether you need to be detained in hospital or not.

Has this happened to you?

. . . . . . . . . . . . . . . . . . . . . . . . . . . . . . . . . . . . . . . . . . . . . . . . . . . . . . . . . . . . . . . . . . . . . . . . . . . . . . . . . . . . . . . .

. . . . . . . . . . . . . . . . . . . . . . . . . . . . . . . . . . . . . . . . . . . . . . . . . . . . . . . . . . . . . . . . . . . . . . . . . . . . . . . . . . . . . . . .

If so how did you feel?

. . . . . . . . . . . . . . . . . . . . . . . . . . . . . . . . . . . . . . . . . . . . . . . . . . . . . . . . . . . . . . . . . . . . . . . . . . . . . . . . . . . . . . . .

. . . . . . . . . . . . . . . . . . . . . . . . . . . . . . . . . . . . . . . . . . . . . . . . . . . . . . . . . . . . . . . . . . . . . . . . . . . . . . . . . . . . . . . .

. . . . . . . . . . . . . . . . . . . . . . . . . . . . . . . . . . . . . . . . . . . . . . . . . . . . . . . . . . . . . . . . . . . . . . . . . . . . . . . . . . . . . . . .

What emotions do you think your family felt?

. . . . . . . . . . . . . . . . . . . . . . . . . . . . . . . . . . . . . . . . . . . . . . . . . . . . . . . . . . . . . . . . . . . . . . . . . . . . . . . . . . . . . . . .

. . . . . . . . . . . . . . . . . . . . . . . . . . . . . . . . . . . . . . . . . . . . . . . . . . . . . . . . . . . . . . . . . . . . . . . . . . . . . . . . . . . . . . . .

Many families feel grief stricken when this situation happens, but they would only use it as a last resort if they believe that you are too unwell to make a decision or that an admission into hospital in your best interests or for the safety of others. Don't be angry with them because they are helping you, although you might not think it at the time.

When you are feeling well, start to complete the crisis action plan on page 114 and give it to your family and health professional (e.g. A & E and mental health worker) if you feel suicidal. When feeling suicidal, rate your suicidal urges so that others can monitor your emotional state.

When feeling suicidal you may be unable to communicate your emotions verbally, but the crisis action plan will give others guidelines on how to support and help you cope during a crisis situation. It will also alert others to your distress allowing people who care about you to give the right support and help.

Again have some patience with your family and give them time to understand you and your disorder and remember that they want to help you but don't know how to. Help your family, friends and health professionals find ways of working together in supporting you and your needs.

# ▶ CRISIS ACTION PLAN

Due to experiencing some suicidal thoughts I am having difficulty expressing my needs to you, but I would like some help and support from you.

My name is: ......................................................................

My address is: ...................................................................

My GP is: ........................................................................

The current medication that I am taking is: .........................................

Please could you contact the following people?

.......................................................................telephone:

.......................................................................telephone:

.......................................................................telephone:

I am at present experiencing suicidal thoughts and on a scale of 0–10 with 10 being the strongest urge I feel are:

Time: ............................... scale of urge: ...............................

Time: ............................... scale of urge: ...............................

Time: ............................... scale of urge: ...............................

Thoughts that are going through my head are:.......................................
................................................................................

Emotions that I am feeling are: ....................................................
................................................................................

I am particularly at high risk when: ...............................................
................................................................................

The following treatments have been helpful to me in the past are: ....................
................................................................................

It would also be helpful if you could: .............................................

It is not helpful to me if: .......................................................
................................................................................

Signed: ............................. Witness

signature:..................

| Thank you for your time and understanding |
| --- |

## ▶ Wheel of 'suicidal ideas' end-of-session Questionnaire

What three important things have you learnt and will take away with you from this session (you may need to browse through the session again to jog your memory).

1 . . . . . . . . . . . . . . . . . . . . . . . . . . . . . . . . . . . . . . . . . . . . . . . . . . . . . . . . . . . . . . . . . . . . . . . . . . . . . . . . . . . . . . . . . . . . . . . . . . . . . . . . . . . . . . . . . . . . . . . . . . . . . . . . . . . . . . . . . . . . . . . . . . . . . . . . . . . . . . . . . . . . . . . . . . . . . . . . . . . . . . . . . . . . . . . . . . . . . . . . . . . . . . . . . . . . . . . . . . . . . . . . . . . . . . . . . . . . . . . . . . . . . . . . . . . . . . . . . . . . . . . . . . . . . . . . . . . . . . . . . . . . . . . . . . . . . . . . . . . . . . . . . . . . . . . . . . . . . . . . . . . . . . . . . . . . . . . . . . . . . . . . . . . . . . . . . . . . . . . . . . . . . . . . . . . . . . . . . . . . . . . . . . . . . . . . . . . . . . . . . . . . . . . . . . . . . . . . . . . . . . . . . . . . . . . . . . . . . . . . . . . . . . . . . . . . . . . . . . . . . . . . . . . . . .

2 . . . . . . . . . . . . . . . . . . . . . . . . . . . . . . . . . . . . . . . . . . . . . . . . . . . . . . . . . . . . . . . . . . . . . . . . . . . . . . . . . . . . . . . . . . . . . . . . . . . . . . . . . . . . . . . . . . . . . . . . . . . . . . . . . . . . . . . . . . . . . . . . . . . . . . . . . . . . . . . . . . . . . . . . . . . . . . . . . . . . . . . . . . . . . . . . . . . . . . . . . . . . . . . . . . . . . . . . . . . . . . . . . . . . . . . . . . . . . . . . . . . . . . . . . . . . . . . . . . . . . . . . . . . . . . . . . . . . . . . . . . . . . . . . . . . . . . . . . . . . . . . . . . . . . . . . . . . . . . . . . . . . . . . . . . . . . . . . . . . . . . . . . . . . . . . . . . . . . . . . . . . . . . . . . . . . . . . . . . . . . . . . . . . .

3 . . . . . . . . . . . . . . . . . . . . . . . . . . . . . . . . . . . . . . . . . . . . . . . . . . . . . . . . . . . . . . . . . . . . . . . . . . . . . . . . . . . . . . . . . . . . . . . . . . . . . . . . . . . . . . . . . . . . . . . . . . . . . . . . . . . . . . . . . . . . . . . . . . . . . . . . . . . . . . . . . . . . . . . . . . . . . . . . . . . . . . . . . . . . . . . . . . . . . . . . . . . . . . . . . . . . . . . . . . . . . . . . . . . . . . . . . . . . . . . . . . . . . . . . . . . . . . . . . . . . . . . . . . . . . . . . . . . . . . . . . . . . . . . . . . . . . . . . . . . . . . . . . . . . . . . . . . . . . . . . . . . . . . . . . . . . . . . . . . . . . . . . . . . . . . . . . . . . . . . . . . . . . . . . . . . . . . . . . . . . . . . . . . . .

## ▶ ABANDONMENT

Abandonment issues are a symptom of your inner distress. The following session is not meant as a form of treatment, but gives ideas of coping strategies to work alongside talking therapies. Hopefully this session will help you to understand why you are the way you are so that you can seek further help through talking therapy.

If you have issues with feelings of abandonment how differently do you think your life would be if you were able to cope with these feelings more effectively?

. . . . . . . . . . . . . . . . . . . . . . . . . . . . . . . . . . . . . . . . . . . . . . . . . . . . . . . . . . . . . . . . . . . . . . . . . . . . . . . . .

. . . . . . . . . . . . . . . . . . . . . . . . . . . . . . . . . . . . . . . . . . . . . . . . . . . . . . . . . . . . . . . . . . . . . . . . . . . . . . . . .

. . . . . . . . . . . . . . . . . . . . . . . . . . . . . . . . . . . . . . . . . . . . . . . . . . . . . . . . . . . . . . . . . . . . . . . . . . . . . . . . .

What would be important to you about this?

. . . . . . . . . . . . . . . . . . . . . . . . . . . . . . . . . . . . . . . . . . . . . . . . . . . . . . . . . . . . . . . . . . . . . . . . . . . . . . . . .

. . . . . . . . . . . . . . . . . . . . . . . . . . . . . . . . . . . . . . . . . . . . . . . . . . . . . . . . . . . . . . . . . . . . . . . . . . . . . . . . .

Nothing will happen unless we create a chance for it to come about.

It may be helpful for you to browse through Session 3 on page 33 to recap on the symptoms of abandonment.

Below we will be looking at a 'wheel of abandonment' where each segment represents skills you can learn in relation to feelings of abandonment. Consider each segment, rating each one from 0–10 with 10 being the most difficult skill to manage when feeling left out or abandoned.

## WHEEL OF ABANDONMENT

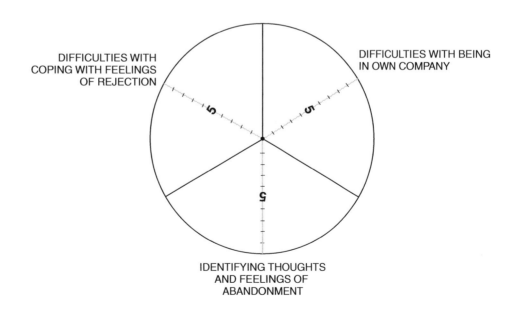

DIFFICULTIES WITH
COPING WITH FEELINGS
OF REJECTION

DIFFICULTIES WITH BEING
IN OWN COMPANY

IDENTIFYING THOUGHTS
AND FEELINGS OF
ABANDONMENT

## IDENTIFYING THOUGHTS AND FEELINGS OF ABANDONMENT

It is common for someone who suffers from a Borderline Personality Disorder to have deep subconscious issues with abandonment. It is a complicated human problem that is overwhelmingly deep rooted in fear and insecurity.

Describe how strong these feelings that you will be left alone with no one to care for you are?

.........................................................................................

.........................................................................................

John Bowlby (1973) claims that whilst growing up, we all need to form a close and affectionate bond with another person; this is the core of all human development and A. L Scroufe (1997) stated that it is through these attachments that an infant will learn how to regulate their emotions.

Maslow (1943) stated that we all have needs that have to be met, particularly when we are children, when we rely on someone else until we are old enough to meet them for ourselves.

If a child's basic emotional needs are not met whilst growing up they learn not to trust others to 'be there' and/or to rely on anyone to make them feel safe and secure. As already stated Bowlby highlighted that although the attachment theory is mainly emphasised in childhood it continues throughout our lives.

The common triggers of abandonment for sufferers of Borderline Personality Disorder are when you feel that you have upset someone in some way and then fear they are going to leave you.

You need to explore with your doctor or nurse what your trigger points are, that is, which feelings or situations are more likely to make you feel abandoned:

.........................................................................................

.........................................................................................

Think of a situation when you last felt left out or abandoned:

**When** ..................................................................................

**Where** ................................................................................

**What happened** ......................................................................

.........................................................................................

Are you aware of any physical sensations prior to your feelings of being abandoned?

- racing heart and palpitations
- stomach ache
- sweating
- tense muscles – e.g. shoulders, neck, back and head
- feeling faint and dizzy
- shallow breathing – breathlessness, fast breathing

- redness in face
- eyes seem blurred
- dry mouth
- feeling nausea
- shaking
- headache.

List below your physical sensations:

........................................................................................................

You can recognise the above as warning signs that you may be reaching the point where you will be feeling overwhelmed with fear and feeling vulnerable.

What thoughts were running through your head when you felt that someone was going to leave you?

........................................................................................................

........................................................................................................

If this happens again then stop and think of it as a red traffic light – STOP

---

It would be helpful to say to yourself:

**When I experience**.......................................................................................

........................................................................................................

........................................................................................................

'I will stop and think for a moment where this is going to lead me'.

---

### DIFFICULTIES WITH COPING WITH FEELINGS OF REJECTION

In Session 2 the amygdale, which is an almond-shaped structure in the brain was briefly discussed (page 18) and is said to be linked with the overwhelming feelings you at times experience when you are in a situation when you fear that others may leave you.

This is because the first and foremost emotion that we are born with is fear, and a baby's first fear is to be left on its own, because if it did not have anyone to feed and keep it safe and well, it would not survive. This amygdala responsibility is to be alert to any situation that may cause you to be abandoned which will trigger off feelings of anxiety.

Anderson (1999) stated that the amygdala stores memories from our childhood and anything that reminds you of any distressing past events where you felt alone and neglected will set off alarm bells for you and will push you into a sense of emergency causing you to feel anxious and afraid. Anderson also stated that this is because the amygdala is not capable of knowing that you have grown up and that you do not necessarily need someone to feed you and that you would not die if you were left on your own.

Also, if the attachment process (Bowlby, 1973) has been interrupted for whatever reason whilst you were growing up can also cause you to experience intense overwhelming feelings of rejection and loneliness when you think that people are unhappy with you and are going to leave you or not love you any more.

Do you often feel overwhelmed with intense feelings when you feel that others do not like you? If so describe what it feels like.

. . . . . . . . . . . . . . . . . . . . . . . . . . . . . . . . . . . . . . . . . . . . . . . . . . . . . . . . . . . . . . . . . . . . . . . . . . . . . . . . . . . . . . . . . .

. . . . . . . . . . . . . . . . . . . . . . . . . . . . . . . . . . . . . . . . . . . . . . . . . . . . . . . . . . . . . . . . . . . . . . . . . . . . . . . . . . . . . . . . . .

Those who suffer from borderline personality disorder are extremely sensitive to others' emotions and at times may overact to feelings of rejection for which may not have been intended.

Have you ever experienced feeling rejected regarding what someone had said or done to you and later learnt that your belief was wrong?

. . . . . . . . . . . . . . . . . . . . . . . . . . . . . . . . . . . . . . . . . . . . . . . . . . . . . . . . . . . . . . . . . . . . . . . . . . . . . . . . . . . . . . . . . .

. . . . . . . . . . . . . . . . . . . . . . . . . . . . . . . . . . . . . . . . . . . . . . . . . . . . . . . . . . . . . . . . . . . . . . . . . . . . . . . . . . . . . . . . . .

Do you find yourself searching for someone to make you feel safe and secure by forming intense relationships in the hope of resolving the unmet needs from your past and then feel scared out of your wits if you are ignored or neglected by them?

. . . . . . . . . . . . . . . . . . . . . . . . . . . . . . . . . . . . . . . . . . . . . . . . . . . . . . . . . . . . . . . . . . . . . . . . . . . . . . . . . . . . . . . . . .

. . . . . . . . . . . . . . . . . . . . . . . . . . . . . . . . . . . . . . . . . . . . . . . . . . . . . . . . . . . . . . . . . . . . . . . . . . . . . . . . . . . . . . . . . .

. . . . . . . . . . . . . . . . . . . . . . . . . . . . . . . . . . . . . . . . . . . . . . . . . . . . . . . . . . . . . . . . . . . . . . . . . . . . . . . . . . . . . . . . . .

If you are giving out messages to others that you desperately want closeness and intimacy and are forever searching for someone to care for you it is important that you:

- learn how to be who you are
- to be OK with that person
- learn how to be alone with yourself
- learn how to meet your own emotional needs.

When you have identified physical sensations on page 133 the following steps may be helpful to you:

**Step One**

When you have felt a bit uneasy but don't know why or you experience any physical sensations, tell yourself this is how you are feeling or approach someone you trust and tell them.

Is this something you feel you could do? What is your plan for Step One if you experience the above sensations?

. . . . . . . . . . . . . . . . . . . . . . . . . . . . . . . . . . . . . . . . . . . . . . . . . . . . . . . . . . . . . . . . . . . . . . . . . . . . . . .

. . . . . . . . . . . . . . . . . . . . . . . . . . . . . . . . . . . . . . . . . . . . . . . . . . . . . . . . . . . . . . . . . . . . . . . . . . . . . . .

**Step Two**

Try and trace this this back to where the uncomfortable feeling originally came from, for example, it may be someone said something to you that made you feel uneasy.

Can you think of an occasion when an uncomfortable situation triggered a physical sensation?

. . . . . . . . . . . . . . . . . . . . . . . . . . . . . . . . . . . . . . . . . . . . . . . . . . . . . . . . . . . . . . . . . . . . . . . . . . . . . . .

. . . . . . . . . . . . . . . . . . . . . . . . . . . . . . . . . . . . . . . . . . . . . . . . . . . . . . . . . . . . . . . . . . . . . . . . . . . . . . .

**Step Three**

Tell yourself that you are going to put this uncomfortable feeling on hold until you can give yourself space to deal with it, practice mindfulness and focusing on your five senses (pages 85 and 89).

What other activities could you do to distract yourself from this difficult feeling?

. . . . . . . . . . . . . . . . . . . . . . . . . . . . . . . . . . . . . . . . . . . . . . . . . . . . . . . . . . . . . . . . . . . . . . . . . . . . . . .

. . . . . . . . . . . . . . . . . . . . . . . . . . . . . . . . . . . . . . . . . . . . . . . . . . . . . . . . . . . . . . . . . . . . . . . . . . . . . . .

**Step Four**

When you think the time is right talk to someone about this feeling or if you think you can manage this feeling on your own deal with it yourself. You might learn that this is a feeling of abandonment and the process will help you to understand your fears and concerns.

**Step Five**

When you have understood this feeling of abandonment let it go and take care of yourself by using any of the strategies on page 90 and browsing through your comforting tool box on page 91.

Only after you have worked through your emotions will you have room to learn how to love and be loved, to know others and to trust others to know you (Mahari, 1999).

Speak to your psychologist to help you through this journey.

## DIFFICULTIES WITH BEING IN YOUR OWN COMPANY

If you suffer from Borderline Personality Disorder you may have difficulty in being comfortable in your own company. Is this true for you? If so describe why?

. . . . . . . . . . . . . . . . . . . . . . . . . . . . . . . . . . . . . . . . . . . . . . . . . . . . . . . . . . . . . . . . . . . . . . . . . . . . . . .

. . . . . . . . . . . . . . . . . . . . . . . . . . . . . . . . . . . . . . . . . . . . . . . . . . . . . . . . . . . . . . . . . . . . . . . . . . . . . . .

It is important that you are not dependent on others to nurture or make you feel good about yourself, because you can do this for yourself and this will help you to find the 'real' you in the process. Spending more 'time out' with yourself in pleasurable activities will enable you to develop a self contented relationship with yourself which is something you have found difficult up to now. Learning to accept separateness is a step closer to coping with feelings of abandonment and learning how to meet your own emotional needs.

This idea may obviously cause you some anxiety, but let those feelings pass and just think about taking only small steps and work out for yourself a schedule whereby you think of two pleasurable activities you can do a day. Browse through the list below and add more if you want and then complete the 'time out schedule' on page 139.

- lie on your bed and rest your eyes and cuddle a soft toy
- soak in bath
- walk somewhere that has lovely views to look at
- make yourself breakfast in bed
- listen to all different types of music and identify your favourite ones
- paint your nails
- go to the library and browse before choosing a book
- go to bed early and watch TV in bed
- read all the gossip in a magazine
- sit in the garden at night with your coat on and a cup of tea and gaze at the stars
- spend time stroking your pet or someone else's pet
- walk along the beach without your shoes and socks on
- make some sandcastles in the sand
- go and watch a local football match
- go to a car boot sale
- browse in a department store
- go to a theme park and have some fun on the rides
- sit on some swings in the local playground
- borrow a talking library book and listen to the story
- go to the cinema and watch a film
- sit and feed some ducks in a park
- bake some bread when you are in the house alone
- have a facial in a beauty salon
- have a shower and spend time rubbing in lotion all over your body
- go to book shop and have a cup of coffee in their café and look through their bestseller list and consider buying one of them
- meditate
- attend classes to meet new people
- go to museum
- do some gym work
- make yourself a lovely dinner with all the trimmings
- write some notes to people you care about
- sit in church and get some comfort through prayer

- watch a funny DVD
- work on a hobby you are interested in.

Which activities would you be interested in that would give you some 'quality time' on your own?

........................................................................................

........................................................................................

........................................................................................

........................................................................................

........................................................................................

........................................................................................

........................................................................................

| **Become your own best friend** |
| --- |

# ▶ 'TIME OUT' SCHEDULE

Consider two pleasurable activities to do each day and complete one every week.

| Monday | Tuesday | Wednesday | Thursday | Friday | Saturday | Sunday |
|--------|---------|-----------|----------|--------|----------|--------|
|        |         |           |          |        |          |        |
|        |         |           |          |        |          |        |

It is important that you build up the time with yourself gradually, perhaps allocate 15 minutes a day for an activity and when you feel ready, perhaps after a week or so, increase the activity to 30 minutes and so on.

The above suggestions alone are not enough for you to cope with your feelings of abandonment, but these ideas can be helpful if they are working along side talking therapies.

## ▶ Wheel of 'abandonment' end-of-session Questionnaire

What three important things have you learnt and will take away with you from wheel of abandonment (you may need to browse through the session again to jog your memory).

1 ....................................................................................................................
....................................................................................................................
....................................................................................................................
....................................................................................................................
....................................................................................................................
....................................................................................................................
....................................................................................................................
....................................................................................................................
....................................................................................................................
....................................................................................................................

2 ....................................................................................................................
....................................................................................................................
....................................................................................................................
....................................................................................................................
....................................................................................................................
....................................................................................................................
....................................................................................................................
....................................................................................................................
....................................................................................................................

3 ....................................................................................................................
....................................................................................................................
....................................................................................................................
....................................................................................................................
....................................................................................................................
....................................................................................................................
....................................................................................................................
....................................................................................................................
....................................................................................................................

Difficulty in communicating your needs with others within a relationship is a symptom of your inner distress, but the following session is not meant as a form of treatment but gives ideas of alternative coping strategies to work alongside talking therapies. Hopefully, this session will help you to understand why you are the way you are so that you can seek further help through talking therapy.

Do you feel that you have a problem regarding how you relate to others?

. . . . . . . . . . . . . . . . . . . . . . . . . . . . . . . . . . . . . . . . . . . . . . . . . . . . . . . . . . . . . . . . . . . . . . . . . . . . . . .

If you have issues regarding your relationship with others how differently do you think your life would be if you were able to cope with these feelings more effectively?

. . . . . . . . . . . . . . . . . . . . . . . . . . . . . . . . . . . . . . . . . . . . . . . . . . . . . . . . . . . . . . . . . . . . . . . . . . . . . . .

. . . . . . . . . . . . . . . . . . . . . . . . . . . . . . . . . . . . . . . . . . . . . . . . . . . . . . . . . . . . . . . . . . . . . . . . . . . . . . .

What would be important to you about this?

. . . . . . . . . . . . . . . . . . . . . . . . . . . . . . . . . . . . . . . . . . . . . . . . . . . . . . . . . . . . . . . . . . . . . . . . . . . . . . .

. . . . . . . . . . . . . . . . . . . . . . . . . . . . . . . . . . . . . . . . . . . . . . . . . . . . . . . . . . . . . . . . . . . . . . . . . . . . . . .

Nothing will happen unless we create a chance for it to come about.

It might be helpful for you to browse through Session 3 again on page 34 to recap on relationship issues.

Below we will be looking at a 'wheel of relationships' where each segment represents skills you can learn in relation to communication issues. Consider each segment, rating each one from 0–10 with 10 being the most difficult skill for you to manage in regards to relationships with others.

## WHEEL OF RELATIONSHIPS

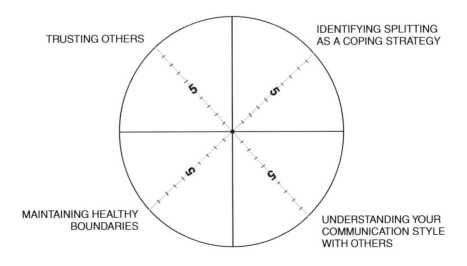

Relationships are connections that exist between two people and are extremely important to us all as no human being can survive being in isolation. It is through these relationships that we pick up unconscious messages on how to trust, respect and communicate with another human being, all of which help put forward a picture of what relationships are really about.

Some sufferers may have had difficult relationships whilst growing up and this would have a profound effect on how they relate to others, due to those unconscious messages relating to trust, respect and communication. This has caused sufferers to have a very complicated view of relationships resulting in:

- lack of trust
- fear and anxiety
- misunderstandings of others' intentions
- anger
- sadness.

## TRUSTING OTHERS

Do you or anyone you know have trouble trusting others?

.................................................................................................................

.................................................................................................................

Why do think that is?

.................................................................................................................

.................................................................................................................

Those who have grown up in an environment whereby they felt safe and secure would find it much easier to trust people, however, those who felt rejected and unsafe whilst growing up would find it much harder to trust others to treat them well.

When you last felt distrustful of someone what went through your mind?

.................................................................................................................

.................................................................................................................

There are times when you are right to be suspicious, but there are also times when you could be mistaken. If you unthinkingly jump to the wrong conclusion it could not only be embarrassing but may cause you to act in ways you may later regret.

Because you are very sensitive to the fear of others abandoning you it may cause you to be hypervigilant for signs that others are going to reject you or are untrustworthy; this may trigger a reaction from you to hit out at others because of your anxiety and distrust.

Have you unmistakably jumped to the wrong conclusion and acted in a way you later regretted?

. . . . . . . . . . . . . . . . . . . . . . . . . . . . . . . . . . . . . . . . . . . . . . . . . . . . . . . . . . . . . . . . . . . . . . . . . . . . .

. . . . . . . . . . . . . . . . . . . . . . . . . . . . . . . . . . . . . . . . . . . . . . . . . . . . . . . . . . . . . . . . . . . . . . . . . . . . .

. . . . . . . . . . . . . . . . . . . . . . . . . . . . . . . . . . . . . . . . . . . . . . . . . . . . . . . . . . . . . . . . . . . . . . . . . . . . .

. . . . . . . . . . . . . . . . . . . . . . . . . . . . . . . . . . . . . . . . . . . . . . . . . . . . . . . . . . . . . . . . . . . . . . . . . . . . .

If this happens again then stop and think of it as a red traffic light – STOP

---

It would be helpful to say to yourself:

**When I experience** . . . . . . . . . . . . . . . . . . . . . . . . . . . . . . . . . . . . . . . . . . . . . . . . . . . . . . . . .

. . . . . . . . . . . . . . . . . . . . . . . . . . . . . . . . . . . . . . . . . . . . . . . . . . . . . . . . . . . . . . . . . . . . . .

. . . . . . . . . . . . . . . . . . . . . . . . . . . . . . . . . . . . . . . . . . . . . . . . . . . . . . . . . . . . . . . . . . . . . .

'I will stop and think for a moment where this is going to lead me'.

---

You could also say to yourself:

- Could I be reading this wrong?
- What other reasons could there be?
- Am I feeling tired and stressed?
- I cannot mind read and know what people are thinking.
- I should use mindfulness and be aware of my five senses around me at this moment to distract me from these negative thoughts.

You could approach others and talk to them about how you feel as we all have times when we feel scared and vulnerable.

Building trust takes time and especially if you have been hurt in the past it can be difficult. If you have trouble trusting anyone, the first step would be to discuss this with your psychologist or mental health worker who will help you to rebuild faith and trust in others.

## IDENTIFYING SPLITTING AS A COPING STRATEGY

Children split their world into being either all good or all bad, for example, there can only be a bad wicked stepmother or a good fairy godmother. Otto Kernberg (1995) stated that as part of our childhood development we learn to take on board these black and white feelings of good/bad and love/hate.

Kernberg's theory claims that there are three stages of development which refer to this type of 'splitting' and it has been suggested that those who suffer from borderline personality disorder may have difficulties moving on to the third stage of his developmental model, which is the self and others being seen as having both good and bad qualities.

Do you think of people as either being either all bad or all good?

..................................................................................................

..................................................................................................

..................................................................................................

Do you have difficulty understanding that someone could be both good and bad?

..................................................................................................

..................................................................................................

Sufferers use this splitting as a type of coping strategy to protect themselves when they are feeling vulnerable, but it can cause many problems in your relationships with others.

Have you felt great admiration and love for someone and then all of a sudden felt intense anger and dislike towards them when a slight disagreement occurs between you both?

..................................................................................................

..................................................................................................

You may also love this workbook because you feel that there is an understanding of what you are going through or you may hate this workbook because you feel regretful about your behaviours and tell yourself you are a bad person and that you do not want to continue.

Don't worry, this is understandable, but with the support of someone you can trust you will be able to unlearn this coping strategy of splitting and see and be comfortable with the good parts and the bad parts of yourself and others.

## MAINTAINING HEALTHY BOUNDARIES

Sufferers of Borderline Personality Disorder at times rely a great deal on others to help provide them with an identity and to raise their self esteem; seeking desperately for someone who can give them a lot of love and support to fill the black hole and feelings of hopelessness inside them.

Judy Saltarelli (2000) described boundaries as being like a wall that we build up around us; if the wall is built high with no windows or doors no one can hurt you, but the consequences are that you will feel alone and cut off from everyone without any closeness or support. If, on the other hand, the wall is low and weak and lets anyone enter, it leaves you vulnerable to abuse or manipulation.

What Judy suggests is a wall that is made of bricks, but has also a gate and window with a good lock and only you have the key and you decide who to let in or who to lock out.

Describe the wall you have built around yourself:

..................................................................................................

..................................................................................................

..................................................................................................

There are three main types of boundaries: physical, emotional and spiritual.

*Physical boundary rights* include:

- You have the right to say how close you want someone to stand next to you to protect your personal space.
- You have the right to say if your privacy is not being respected, for example, someone reading your personal letters or not knocking on the door when they enter your room.
- You have the right to say who is going to touch you.

*Emotional boundary rights* include:

- You have the right not to sacrifice your plans in order to please others.
- You have the right to have your feelings respected.
- You have the right not to take responsibility for others' feelings.
- You have the right not to let other people's moods dictate your level of happiness.
- You have the right to take responsibility for yourself and not blame others for your problems.
- You have the right to choose how you let people treat you.
- You have the right to set limits on what people say to you.

*Spiritual boundary rights* include:

- You have the right to believe as you do.
- You have the right for others to respect your religion.

Which of the above rights are important to you?

..............................................................................................

..............................................................................................

..............................................................................................

Unhealthy boundaries are generally developed as a result of being brought up in families where appreciation of others' rights was not properly recognised or where the child was not respected as an individual. This causes confusion within individuals because they are unable to recognise where they end and the other person begins.

Those who suffer from Borderline Personality Disorder also have unclear boundaries which cause them to move to and fro between feelings of being swallowed up on the one hand and abandonment on the other. Because sufferers usually have a low self esteem they can be overly dependent on others for approval and are therefore afraid of rejection or conflict with others.

Do you feel that you are dependent on others for approval?

..............................................................................................

..............................................................................................

Unhealthy boundaries are characterised by:

■ Having difficulty saying no for fear of rejection.
■ Having difficulty protecting yourself from physical and emotional troubles.
■ Feeling responsible for others' problems.
■ Allowing others to make decisions and hold the power over you.
■ Putting others' needs before your own needs.
■ Feeling 'needy' towards someone in order that you survive.

Do any of the above apply to you?

...................................................................................................
...................................................................................................
...................................................................................................
...................................................................................................

It is very difficult to set boundaries unless you are able to communicate your needs to others in an open and honest manner. It would be helpful if you described your personal boundaries with an 'I' statement for example:

■ I feel threatened when ........................................................................
■ I feel angry when ...............................................................................
■ I would be happier if............................................................................
■ I would prefer if .................................................................................

Get into the habit of making 'I' statements and complete an 'I' statement below that you could practice on someone today:

'I ....................................................................................................
...................................................................................................
...................................................................................................

Setting boundaries is essential for you to gain some self-confidence and independence.

## UNDERSTANDING YOUR COMMUNICATION STYLE WITH OTHERS

Eric Berne (1961) described three personality styles or ego states to illustrate how we interact with others and explores what goes through our minds during any communication looking at:

■ What drives us to say the things that we do?
■ Why do we say the things that we do?
■ How do we say the things that we do?

Berne named these three ego states as 'parent', 'adult' and 'child' and each ego state is made up of thoughts, feelings and behaviours.

**Parent**

This ego state is the voice of authority which we have copied from our parents, teachers etc. that was ingrained in us all when we were young. There are two parts to this parent ego state which are the 'nurturing parent' and the 'controlling or critical parent' and have a range of expression which can be either negative or positive for example:

- nurturing
- spoiling
- controlling
- critical
- patronising
- finger pointing
- judgemental
- says words like 'you should'
- caring and concerned
- calming
- prejudiced
- domineering
- strongly opinionated
- disciplines
- advises
- guides
- protects.

Name three of the above which describe the nurturing parent ego state:

. . . . . . . . . . . . . . . . . . . . . . . . . . . . . . . . . . . . . . . . . . . . . . . . . . . . . . . . . . . . . . . . . . . . . . . . . . . . . . . . . . . . .

. . . . . . . . . . . . . . . . . . . . . . . . . . . . . . . . . . . . . . . . . . . . . . . . . . . . . . . . . . . . . . . . . . . . . . . . . . . . . . . . . . . . .

Name three of the above which describe the controlling or critical parent ego state:

. . . . . . . . . . . . . . . . . . . . . . . . . . . . . . . . . . . . . . . . . . . . . . . . . . . . . . . . . . . . . . . . . . . . . . . . . . . . . . . . . . . . .

. . . . . . . . . . . . . . . . . . . . . . . . . . . . . . . . . . . . . . . . . . . . . . . . . . . . . . . . . . . . . . . . . . . . . . . . . . . . . . . . . . . . .

**Adult**

This ego state is the 'grown up' and common sense part of ourselves which enables us to think logically and reflect on the incoming messages we receive during our communication with others. It is also the process by which we keep our parent and child ego states under control by being:

- rational
- reasonable
- assertive

- non threatening
- attentive
- decision making
- logic
- goal setting
- calm
- reasonable
- patient
- problem solver
- reflective
- good listener.

### Child

This ego state is when our behaviours and emotions are replayed from our own childhood. There are two parts to this ego state which are the 'adaptive child' and the 'free child' and both can have both negative and positive behaviour. The *adaptive child* can be cooperative which is described as a positive behaviour; and obedient/defiant which is a negative behaviour.

The *free child* can be spontaneous which is described as a positive behaviour and immature and childish which is a negative behaviour.

- fun loving
- compliant
- rebellious
- manipulative
- creative
- energetic
- polite
- spontaneous
- temper tantrums
- baby talk
- curious
- fearful.

Name three of the above which describe the adaptive ego state:

........................................................................................................

........................................................................................................

Name three of the above which describe the free child ego state:

........................................................................................................

........................................................................................................

Name seven ego states that best describe you, referring to the parent, adult and child ego states described:

..................................................................................................

..................................................................................................

..................................................................................................

..................................................................................................

To highlight how these three ego states link into how we communicate with others it is best to describe a scenario.

Say someone gave you a task to do and after you completed the task their response was 'you are absolutely useless, you should have done it this way and you have got it wrong again', then this statement would be coming from someone's 'controlling or critical parent' style of communication.

You could respond by:

- Saying to yourself 'I am no good because I never get it right so I must be stupid' then this statement would be coming from your 'adaptive child' style of communication.
- Saying to yourself 'this is not helping my self esteem, is there another way I can do this task more successfully', then this statement would be coming from your 'adult' style of communication.

Would the 'adaptive child' or the 'adult' style of communication be more helpful to you?

..................................................................................................

Many of these responses are subconscious and people don't realise that they have a choice on how they communicate with others. Be aware of your and others' styles of communication and try and pick out which ego state they are coming from. If you need help in understanding more about Berne's 'transactional analysis' theory speak to your mental health worker or psychologist.

Due to difficult childhood experiences some sufferers have a complicated view of relationships which causes problems between themselves and their partners, family and friends. During these problematic times those who are close to you are unsure of how to cope with your changeable moods and impulsive behaviour.

What problems have you experienced in regards to your mood or behaviour which has had a negative affect on your relationship with others?

..................................................................................................

..................................................................................................

..................................................................................................

How do you think your partner, family or friend manage with your difficult moods or behaviour?

..................................................................................................

..................................................................................................

Some partners, family and friends might feel:

- Confused by the things you say and do.
- Helpless as they don't know how to help you.
- Frightened by your angry outbursts.
- Afraid of doing the wrong thing.
- A failure as a husband, wife, son, daughter, mother, father or friend.
- Like they want to reduce their contact with you as they don't know what else to do.
- Upset with your constant blaming and distrust.
- Fearful regarding your self harming behaviour.
- Angry and frustrated regarding your impulsive behaviours.
- Alone when they can't reach you emotionally.

Your family and friends at times struggle with your disorder as much as you do, but you need to remember that they are only human and are trying to cope the best way they can with the limited information they have with regard to understanding how your disorder affects you.

Your family and friends may have difficulties coping with your crises and are worried about you, but don't know what to do for the best, because at times they feel damned if they do and damned if they don't give you the right support or response to your distressed emotional needs.

What do you think you need to be doing to work through these difficult times and how it would help strengthen the relationship between yourself and others?

. . . . . . . . . . . . . . . . . . . . . . . . . . . . . . . . . . . . . . . . . . . . . . . . . . . . . . . . . . . . . . . . . . . . . . . . . . . . . . .

. . . . . . . . . . . . . . . . . . . . . . . . . . . . . . . . . . . . . . . . . . . . . . . . . . . . . . . . . . . . . . . . . . . . . . . . . . . . . . .

. . . . . . . . . . . . . . . . . . . . . . . . . . . . . . . . . . . . . . . . . . . . . . . . . . . . . . . . . . . . . . . . . . . . . . . . . . . . . . .

One thing that is helpful for you to recognise is that the emotional pain you experience at times does sooner or later pass eventually.

Can you remember a time when this happened?

. . . . . . . . . . . . . . . . . . . . . . . . . . . . . . . . . . . . . . . . . . . . . . . . . . . . . . . . . . . . . . . . . . . . . . . . . . . . . . .

. . . . . . . . . . . . . . . . . . . . . . . . . . . . . . . . . . . . . . . . . . . . . . . . . . . . . . . . . . . . . . . . . . . . . . . . . . . . . . .

. . . . . . . . . . . . . . . . . . . . . . . . . . . . . . . . . . . . . . . . . . . . . . . . . . . . . . . . . . . . . . . . . . . . . . . . . . . . . . .

What would help you to build comfortable relationships with those who you care about and who care about you?

. . . . . . . . . . . . . . . . . . . . . . . . . . . . . . . . . . . . . . . . . . . . . . . . . . . . . . . . . . . . . . . . . . . . . . . . . . . . . . .

. . . . . . . . . . . . . . . . . . . . . . . . . . . . . . . . . . . . . . . . . . . . . . . . . . . . . . . . . . . . . . . . . . . . . . . . . . . . . . .

. . . . . . . . . . . . . . . . . . . . . . . . . . . . . . . . . . . . . . . . . . . . . . . . . . . . . . . . . . . . . . . . . . . . . . . . . . . . . . .

It would be helpful to work together with your family and prepare a crisis action plan page 128 which will help give your family guidelines on how to help you cope during a crisis situation.

Some sufferers rely on their loved ones to 'mend' them, but your loved ones are not your therapist and are not responsible for your recovery. Working through therapy with your health professional would be a more successful route to your recovery.

'There are three musts that hold us back: I must do well. You must treat me well. And the world must be easy' (Albert Ellis, 2001).

Engaging and remaining in therapy will be an important, but a tough step for you to take because the work with your therapist will not be easy due to the painful issues that you will have to work through, but can you think of any other alterative choices that would help you to heal and get on with your life in a more content and satisfying way?

With the right support and education for both yourself and those who care about you and by working together as a team you will eventually find a pathway which leads you out of this intense emotional pain and guide you to an alternative pathway which brings about some kind of happiness and fulfilment which you all most certainly deserve.

Are you hopeful that you will find a pathway that leads you to a more contented and satisfying relationship with those who are close to you?

. . . . . . . . . . . . . . . . . . . . . . . . . . . . . . . . . . . . . . . . . . . . . . . . . . . . . . . . . . . . . . . . . . . . . . . . . . . . .

. . . . . . . . . . . . . . . . . . . . . . . . . . . . . . . . . . . . . . . . . . . . . . . . . . . . . . . . . . . . . . . . . . . . . . . . . . . . .

'Hope is important because it can make the present moment less difficult to bear. If we can believe that tomorrow will be better, we can bear a hardship today' (Thich Nhat Hanh).

You may need to heal the pain from your past before you embark on a healthy intimate relationship and the most important step you can take towards your recovery is working with a therapist. It is not enough just to learn coping strategies on a thinking level, like when you are working through this workbook; you need in depth psychological intervention on understanding of how to tolerate emotional discomfort and how to manage these difficult emotions more effectively.

It could take you a while, but what would the benefits be for you in the long term?

. . . . . . . . . . . . . . . . . . . . . . . . . . . . . . . . . . . . . . . . . . . . . . . . . . . . . . . . . . . . . . . . . . . . . . . . . . . . .

. . . . . . . . . . . . . . . . . . . . . . . . . . . . . . . . . . . . . . . . . . . . . . . . . . . . . . . . . . . . . . . . . . . . . . . . . . . . .

. . . . . . . . . . . . . . . . . . . . . . . . . . . . . . . . . . . . . . . . . . . . . . . . . . . . . . . . . . . . . . . . . . . . . . . . . . . . .

Susan Anderson (1999) stated that going through the recovery process step by step will help you to discover and strengthen your sense of who you are and you will finally then make a new connection with the world around you.

What three important things have you learnt and will take away with you from this relationship issues session (you may need to browse through the session again to jog your memory).

1 ..............................................................................................

..............................................................................................

..............................................................................................

..............................................................................................

..............................................................................................

..............................................................................................

..............................................................................................

..............................................................................................

..............................................................................................

..............................................................................................

2 ..............................................................................................

..............................................................................................

..............................................................................................

..............................................................................................

..............................................................................................

..............................................................................................

..............................................................................................

..............................................................................................

..............................................................................................

3 ..............................................................................................

..............................................................................................

..............................................................................................

..............................................................................................

..............................................................................................

..............................................................................................

..............................................................................................

..............................................................................................

..............................................................................................

## ► SELF HARMING

Self harming is a symptom of your inner distress and the following session is not meant as a form of treatment, but gives ideas of coping strategies to work alongside talking therapies. Hopefully this session will help you to understand why you are the way you are so that you can seek further help through talking therapy

If you use self harm as a way of coping with difficult emotions how differently do you think your life would be if you did feel the need to self harm?

..................................................................................................

..................................................................................................

What would be important to you about this?

..................................................................................................

..................................................................................................

Nothing will happen unless we create a chance for it to come about.

It might be helpful for you to browse through Session 3 page 35 to recap on this symptom of self harm.

Be aware that when you read literature about self harm it can sometimes trigger urges in some people. If you are one of those people please stop and move on to another session and discuss this wheel with your psychologist or try again later with your keyworker when you feel stronger in your emotions.

Below we will be looking at a 'wheel of self harm' where each segment represents skills you can learn in relation to your self harming. Consider each segment, rating each one from 0–10 with 10 being the most difficult skill to manage when you feel the need to self harm.

## WHEEL OF SELF HARMING

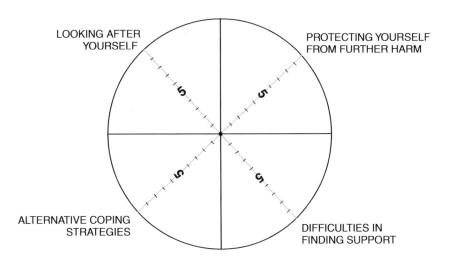

# LOOKING AFTER YOURSELF

As human beings we start out in life as helpless individuals and if the environment we grow up in is 'right' we, like a well nurtured flower may grow tall and reach our full potential. If our environment is not 'right' we may not grow tall or reach our full potential.

Do you feel that you have yet to reach your full potential?

.................................................................................................................

.................................................................................................................

Abraham Maslow (1943) was a psychologist who developed the 'hierarchy of needs' model in which he stated that we are all born with basic needs, but if we do not meet these initial needs it can hinder our lives.

Maslow set up four basic needs:

- physiological needs
- safety needs
- belonging needs
- esteem needs.

When these four basic needs are met Maslow said that we can grow emotionally and develop and give us the skills and confidence to reach our own 'self actualisation'. This means reaching our full potential as a person and feeling comfortable with ourself and our world.

First step – **PHYSIOLOGICAL NEEDS**

What are the basic things you need in life to survive?

.................................................................................................................

.................................................................................................................

These are the very basic needs such as air, water, shelter and warmth, food, sleep. If these needs are not met it could lead you to become physically and mentally unwell.

You can meet some of these basic needs by:

- eating regular healthy meals
- getting regular sleep
- exercising regularly even if it is just a 30 minute walk
- wearing sensible clothes when out
- adequate living accommodation e.g. free from damp
- safe working conditions.

Firstly, in what ways could you take more care of yourself?

.................................................................................................................

.................................................................................................................

Maslow said that if these needs are not met you would experience anxiety and have difficulty moving on to the next step which is 'safety' needs.

Second step – **SAFETY NEEDS**

What needs to happen for you to feel safe?

. . . . . . . . . . . . . . . . . . . . . . . . . . . . . . . . . . . . . . . . . . . . . . . . . . . . . . . . . . . . . . . . . . . . . . . . . . . . . . . . . .

. . . . . . . . . . . . . . . . . . . . . . . . . . . . . . . . . . . . . . . . . . . . . . . . . . . . . . . . . . . . . . . . . . . . . . . . . . . . . . . . . .

All human beings need to be cared for and protected from harm. In the best circumstances if someone feels that they are being held safely by a warm-hearted person who communicates to them without words that they are lovely, good and worthwhile, this will give that person a feeling of self confidence which will last them all their natural life.

Physical safety means freedom from physical harm and such harm can come from other people like abusive spouses etc. If this is something you are currently experiencing, to protect yourself from further harm you might consider living in a safer environment away from any threats. You must seek support from others if this is a decision you are considering.

If you are currently living in an environment where you fear for your physical safety what actions would you consider taking to keep yourself safe?

. . . . . . . . . . . . . . . . . . . . . . . . . . . . . . . . . . . . . . . . . . . . . . . . . . . . . . . . . . . . . . . . . . . . . . . . . . . . . . . . .

. . . . . . . . . . . . . . . . . . . . . . . . . . . . . . . . . . . . . . . . . . . . . . . . . . . . . . . . . . . . . . . . . . . . . . . . . . . . . . . . .

Physical safety also means being free from hurting yourself.

Psychological safety can sometimes mean protection from yourself, for example, the little voice in your head which sometimes criticises you, which may in turn trigger your cycle of self harming behaviour. You will not be able to grow emotionally and move on until you have addressed these safety needs.

Do you have that critical voice sitting on your shoulder?

. . . . . . . . . . . . . . . . . . . . . . . . . . . . . . . . . . . . . . . . . . . . . . . . . . . . . . . . . . . . . . . . . . . . . . . . . . . . . . . . .

. . . . . . . . . . . . . . . . . . . . . . . . . . . . . . . . . . . . . . . . . . . . . . . . . . . . . . . . . . . . . . . . . . . . . . . . . . . . . . . . .

You need to learn positive self affirmations (nice things to say to yourself), for example:

- I am a caring and loving person.
- I deserve to accept myself as someone unique.
- Today I am calm and confident.
- Today I feel good.
- My life has a purpose.
- I deserve to love myself unconditionally.
- I accept and love myself for the fact that I exist.

Can you think of other positive self affirmations that you could use and make them into cards and put them around your home e.g. mirror or put them in your purse or wallet?

..........................................................................................................

..........................................................................................................

..........................................................................................................

Maslow suggested that only when we feel comfortable and safe, will we be able to move to the next step of meeting our next basic need, the need to belong.

### Third step – A NEED TO BELONG

Human beings need to feel a sense of belonging and acceptance; they also need to love and be loved by others which could be a marriage, friendship, family members or others. In the absence of these factors, many people will become at risk of suffering from loneliness and depression.

Do you have a deep need to belong?

..........................................................................................................

..........................................................................................................

All of us have a need for someone to:

- share and respect our feelings
- share our worries
- be cared for by others
- be given affection.

If the above needs are met it would indicate that we are valued as a person and our existence would matter to someone else and this would give us a sense of belonging.

Those who suffer from Borderline Personality Disorder often have been abandoned either physically or emotionally as children and have not yet had this need satisfied and hence they remain terrified of abandonment in adulthood as mentioned on page 132.

Maslow highlighted that these needs involve both giving and receiving love. If you successfully work through these issues you would then be able to move up on to the next stage and that is meeting our next basic need and that is the need for self esteem.

### Fourth step–SELF ESTEEM NEEDS

Self esteem is about how people feel about themselves and they get esteem by how they judge themselves and by what others think of them. All humans have a need to be appreciated, respected and valued as a person.

Do you feel valued and respected?

..........................................................................................................

..........................................................................................................

Those who suffer from Borderline Personality Disorder have often not known what it feels like to be appreciated and valued as a child and hence often search endlessly for praise and a feeling of being special which they never received when they were young.

If these needs were not met you may experience feelings of worthlessness and helplessness and you may be stuck at this stage and not be able to move on to the final stage of Maslow's hierarchy and that is self actualisation.

There are ways that can help if you become unstuck and this involves looking after your emotional needs by:

- Finding ways of nurturing and pampering yourself e.g. have relaxing bath with oils.
- Seeking out social interaction e.g. phone call, visit a friend or family.
- Doing at least one fun thing a day.
- Rewarding yourself when you have accomplished something difficult e.g. if you have managed to stop yourself from self harming on occasions.

Self care is a skill you must learn if you want to recover, but at first it might feel a bit strange and difficult, but the aim is for you to do at least one caring thing for yourself every day until it becomes natural and comfortable.

If you start to care for yourself it will help you to respect and value yourself and your body more and you will be less likely to want to harm yourself.

### Fifth step – ACHIEVING SELF ACTUALISATION

Self actualisation means reaching our potential as a human being. That is, finding a purpose to our lives and feeling happy and content to be who we are. It is also pursuing one's heart of desire and becoming the best one can be.

Self-actualisation is a need that is so often never fulfilled by most people because they are so caught up in their attempts to accomplish the first four basic needs.

Does it help you to know that if particular needs were not met (according to Maslow) when you were young it could have a profound effect on how you see the world when you get older?

Where on the hierarchy are you being 'held up'?

..............................................................................

..............................................................................

To find oneself is to take that first step and with support from others climb up steadily through the remaining steps two, three and four until you reach the very top step when you find contentment with yourself and have no need to use self harming as a way of dealing with difficult emotions.

There may be times when you stumble or take three steps forward and two steps backward, but no matter how far you fall down backwards your next steps will be easier because you have already travelled so far and you know the way.

If you have identified an area of needs with which you are stuck what can you do about it?

..............................................................................................

..............................................................................................

Firstly, you need to accept that if your needs were not met when you were growing up it was not in any way or form your fault and understand that when you were young you did not have the words to explain how you were feeling and so you locked yourself away in a deep place inside yourself for protection.

The inner child now needs to stop hiding away and come out, but you won't do that until you feel safe, which is understandable. The truth is that the only person now who can meet your true inner needs is YOU.

Secondly, learn ways of being there for yourself which means taking care of yourself and the child that is hiding within you.

Write a letter to yourself about the things that make you proud of yourself and what you have managed to achieve despite your past. List below:

..............................................................................................

..............................................................................................

Before you go to bed each night write a list of things you have achieved that day and tell yourself how proud you are.

List five things that make you happy:

> I...........................................................................................
>
> 2...........................................................................................
>
> 3...........................................................................................
>
> 4...........................................................................................
>
> 5...........................................................................................

Thirdly, get support from others to help you stop self harming because in the long run it only causes you more emotional problems.

> Remember that you are special and you deserve it.

The United Kingdom has the highest rates of self harm in Europe with 170,000 attending Accident and Emergency departments a year for incidents of self harm (Samaritans, 2006). This does not include those who don't seek out medical help.

Staying in an abusive relationship, anorexia, bulimia and being addicted to illicit drugs or alcohol are also seen forms of self harming behaviours. For this workbook the self harming behaviour which will be discussed is cutting and drug overdosing.

**Cutting**

The skin can be seen as a boundary when it communicates what is happening both on the inside and the outside of someone's body; that there is somehow a relationship between your skin and how you feel within yourself (*Nursing Times*, January 2002).

What did you learn at school about your skin?

..............................................................................................................

..............................................................................................................

..............................................................................................................

Your skin provides:

- An outside covering and protection for your body, without this covering all your bones, muscles and organs would fall out all over the place.
- Helps keep your body at the right temperature.
- Allows you to have a sense of touch.
- Helps to keep out infection.

Your skin is made of three main layers of tissue:

- epidermis;
- dermis;
- subcutaneous fat.

Your top layer of skin is called the *epidermis* and does not contain any blood vessels and is about the thickness of a piece of paper and is always forming new skin from cell division.

The second layer is called the *dermis*; it contains blood vessels, nerves, roots of your hair and sweat glands.

The third layer is the called the *subcutaneous fat* which stores fat and insulates your body and it contains larger blood vessels and nerves. This layer lies on the muscle and bones where your tendons and ligaments are and to cut into the deeper layers of your skin could cause you many problems:

There are some medical concerns for people who cut themselves:

■ **Infection** An infection to the wound will cause swelling, redness and have an infected discharge.

■ **Tendon and ligament damage** If the cut is deep the underlying muscle (dark red in colour) and tendons (white cords) may be exposed which will result in loss of movement.

■ **Nerve damage** Nerves are fragile and not easy to see when cutting, but if damaged will cause loss of feeling in that area and are unlikely to repair themselves.

■ **Haemorrhage and shock** Haemorrhage is loss of blood which if left untreated your body will go into shock which is a life-threatening condition.

As you can see cutting can be a risky business, but most people who cut have no real intention of permanently maiming or killing themselves; although they may accidentally do so.

During the act of self harm there is usually no pain experienced, this is because the body releases endorphins which provide pain relief and reduce anxiety (Favazza, 1996).

If at any time you are concerned about your wound you should speak to your doctor or visit your local accident and emergency department.

It is accepted that self injury is a way of coping for some people at times and some doctors encourage harm minimisation whereby they give advice on safer ways of self harming which will limit serious damage until more adaptive coping skills have been learnt. This does not mean they condone or encourage self harm, but it is about facing reality regarding maximising safety in the event of self harm. Speak to your doctor or nurse about this.

You may have several reasons to continue cutting, but also at this moment you may have no reason to stop. Seek help from mental health professionals. There are also self help contact numbers at the end of this workbook.

One other problem with cutting is that it leaves a scar and this can cause many uncomfortable questions from other people.

How do you feel about your scars?

.............................................................................................

.............................................................................................

Sometimes it is possible to hide the scars, for example, long sleeves and concealer make up. Good wound care heals scars but there is nothing that can make the scar go away completely. Plastic surgery, skin graphs and other treatments can only change the shape, appearance and location of it and is also very expensive.

**Drug overdosing**

A drug overdose is the accidental or intentional use of a drug in an amount that is higher than the body can tolerate. If a drug is taken in combination with other drugs or with alcohol, then, even if this drug is normally considered safe, it can cause death or serious long-term consequences.

Taking an overdose may cause you to:

- feel nausea
- vomit
- feel dizzy
- feel drowsy
- feel confused about your surroundings
- have breathing problems
- chest pains.

If you have taken too many tablets than you should have, it is important that you seek medical help immediately. This is because some drugs can do extensive damage to your organs before any symptoms develop.

There can be serious consequences of drug overdoses:

- Kidney failure which may mean you need kidney dialysis for the rest of your life.
- Liver failure which may mean you need a liver transplant for you to recover.
- Your heart and lungs may stop working.

When you go to hospital take the overdosed drug container with you so that medical staff will know the correct course of action on how to treat you. Death can happen in almost any drug overdose situation, particularly if treatment is not started immediately. Think about seeking help and support before you reach out for substances and objects to harm yourself.

## ALTERNATIVE HEALTHY COPING SKILLS

Before you can develop alternative coping strategies you need to have more self awareness of what is happening inside and outside your body prior to any self harming actions. Recap on the reasons why you self harm on page 35.

I self harm because:

.............................................................................................

.............................................................................................

.............................................................................................

The next stage is recognising any physical sensations you might have prior to self harm:

What physical sensations do you experience prior to having self harming urges?

- racing heart and palpitations

- stomach ache
- sweating
- tense muscles – e.g. shoulders, neck, back and head
- feeling faint and dizzy
- shallow breathing – breathlessness, fast breathing
- redness in face
- eyes seem blurred
- dry mouth
- feeling nausea
- shaking
- headache.

List below your physical sensations:

. . . . . . . . . . . . . . . . . . . . . . . . . . . . . . . . . . . . . . . . . . . . . . . . . . . . . . . . . . . . . . . . . . . . . . . . . . . . . . . . . . . . .

You can recognise the above as warning signs that you may be reaching the point where you will want to harm yourself.

You may then next experience a thought that will your make urges stronger:

. . . . . . . . . . . . . . . . . . . . . . . . . . . . . . . . . . . . . . . . . . . . . . . . . . . . . . . . . . . . . . . . . . . . . . . . . . . . . . . . . . . . .

. . . . . . . . . . . . . . . . . . . . . . . . . . . . . . . . . . . . . . . . . . . . . . . . . . . . . . . . . . . . . . . . . . . . . . . . . . . . . . . . . . . . .

If this happens then stop and think of it as a red traffic light – STOP

---

It would be helpful to say to yourself:

**When I experience** . . . . . . . . . . . . . . . . . . . . . . . . . . . . . . . . . . . . . . . . . . . . . . . . . . . . . . . . . . . . . . . . .

. . . . . . . . . . . . . . . . . . . . . . . . . . . . . . . . . . . . . . . . . . . . . . . . . . . . . . . . . . . . . . . . . . . . . . . . . . . . . . . .

. . . . . . . . . . . . . . . . . . . . . . . . . . . . . . . . . . . . . . . . . . . . . . . . . . . . . . . . . . . . . . . . . . . . . . . . . . . . . . . .

'I will stop and think for a moment where this is going to lead me'.

---

To stop yourself from self harming is easier said than done though, because at present you are using a well learned behaviour of yours to control your extreme negative emotions; and it is something you may continue to want to use because basically it gives you instant relief by allowing you to release your pain and tension and it makes you feel better straight away. But what does it do for you in the long run?

. . . . . . . . . . . . . . . . . . . . . . . . . . . . . . . . . . . . . . . . . . . . . . . . . . . . . . . . . . . . . . . . . . . . . . . . . . . . . . . . . . . . .

. . . . . . . . . . . . . . . . . . . . . . . . . . . . . . . . . . . . . . . . . . . . . . . . . . . . . . . . . . . . . . . . . . . . . . . . . . . . . . . . . . . . .

It can make you feel worse, but the solution is for you to learn, with support from others, how to tolerate difficult emotions without hurting yourself. To gain some influence over your own life you are going to have to somehow deal with these difficult emotions head on, but an important thing to remember is that each time you manage to do this successfully these feelings will eventually lose their power. You cannot do this alone so it is very important that you seek professional help.

If the time is not right for you at the moment to stop harming yourself don't worry, but there will eventually be a time and until then still try learning ways of reducing your self harming behaviour or practicing other different ways of coping with your feelings.

Have you made a decision regarding your self harming behaviour?

If so what have you decided and why?

.................................................................................

.................................................................................

.................................................................................

If you have decided to stop self harming you need to be aware that during this process you will at times feel frightened, frustrated and very anxious. This is why it is very important that you seek support from people who you trust and can rely on.

Feelings also play a major part in why you self harm so try and identify which emotion you are feeling. Prior to any self harming ask yourself, am I feeling:

Angry.................................................................................

Empty.................................................................................

Guilty.................................................................................

Lonely.................................................................................

Afraid.................................................................................

Ashamed.................................................................................

Sad.................................................................................

Other feelings.................................................................................

Some sufferers are unable to put their feeling into words and don't even know the reason why they self harm because the action itself is so automatic that this understanding has got lost.

In order to develop other coping strategies you need to learn how to cope with uncomfortable feelings (even if you cannot name them) like those mentioned above to make some sense of why you do it. Discuss this with your mental health worker or psychologist.

Understanding why you may feel like self harming is one way of coping with specific feelings. There may be different reasons why you self harm each time depending on what thought and feeling it is that has overwhelmed you:

■ You feel angry or anxious

■ You feel low in your mood and on the whole unhappy

■ You need to see blood to check that you are alive

■ You feel that you need to focus and concentrate on something other than your uncomfortable and difficult feelings

Below are some suggestions of safer alternative coping strategies. Some sufferers have said that they have been helped by them in the past, but some may not be for you. Again discuss them with your mental health worker or psychologist.

Alternative coping strategies for when you *feel angry or anxious*:

*Housework:*

■ hoover the house

■ wash up

■ scrub kitchen floor

■ clean the bathroom

■ spring clean kitchen cupboards

■ bang pots and pans

■ tidy your wardrobe

■ rearrange your room.

*Get out of the house:*

■ go for a brisk walk to the park

■ break up any sticks you find on the way

■ kick leaves

■ go on the swings

■ walk along the beach

■ do some gardening.

*Do some exercise:*

■ go to the gym

■ do some press ups

■ hit a punch bag

■ do some floor exercises

■ dance around the room to a disco song

■ go swimming

■ tear up a cardboard box

■ rip up some old rags

■ tear up newspapers

■ use Play-Doh™.

*Wind down your feelings:*

- talk to someone you trust
- have a bath or shower
- pop bubble wrap
- write
- draw or scribble in journal
- have a good cry.

The idea behind using the above strategies is that when you are angry you have a lot of pent up emotions that need to be released; but by attempting any of the above you will use up a lot of this energy by doing other activities and you will be less likely to want to self harm yourself.

What suggestions above would you be interested in trying if you experienced any angry feelings prior to you wanting to self harming?

. . . . . . . . . . . . . . . . . . . . . . . . . . . . . . . . . . . . . . . . . . . . . . . . . . . . . . . . . . . . . . . . . . . . . . . . . . . . . . . . . . . . . . .

. . . . . . . . . . . . . . . . . . . . . . . . . . . . . . . . . . . . . . . . . . . . . . . . . . . . . . . . . . . . . . . . . . . . . . . . . . . . . . . . . . . . . . .

. . . . . . . . . . . . . . . . . . . . . . . . . . . . . . . . . . . . . . . . . . . . . . . . . . . . . . . . . . . . . . . . . . . . . . . . . . . . . . . . . . . . . . .

Alternative coping strategies for when you **feel low in your mood or are feeling unhappy** as already mentioned on page 90–91.

*Rest your mind:*

- have a relaxing bubble bath
- massage body lotion and oils all over your body
- curl up in bed and listening to calming music
- call a friend and chat about nothing in particular
- watch a soppy film, watch a funny film
- watch cartoons
- get yourself a warm drink and curl up on the settee with a cuddly toy
- ask someone for a cuddle
- walk in the countryside
- read a book
- stroke an animal
- sunbathe in the sun
- sit by the beach and listen to the waves
- wear something that makes you feel good
- do your make up
- give yourself a facial
- relax and close your eyes and breathe slowly
- treat yourself to something nice to eat
- walk a dog
- hug yourself
- practise mindfulness.

*Keep busy:*

- draw a picture of yourself using brightly coloured pens
- buy a colouring book and some pencils
- make a collage and glue all different materials and use coloured pencils
- make up a story and type it out
- write a letter to friends
- write a poem
- pursue any hobbies you might have
- make a present for a friend
- open a dictionary and learn a new word
- do a crossword
- learn to play solitaire card games
- write your feelings in a journal
- do some finger painting with food, for example, ice cream or jam.

What suggestions above would you be interested in trying if you experienced feeling low in your mood prior to you wanting to self harm?

...................................................................................................

...................................................................................................

...................................................................................................

Alternative coping strategies for when you want to **feel focused**:

- hold an ice cube in your hand and squeeze it hard
- bite on a lemon
- wear an elastic band around your wrist and snap it when you have an urge to self harm
- jump around
- stamp your feet
- chew something that tastes hot or nasty
- put your finger in ice cream
- put your hands under cold water
- focus on one thing and describe it as if you were blind
- eat a chocolate bar
- name three things you can hear, see, smell and touch
- play a game on the computer
- find something in the room and write a list of 20 things that would be a good description of it.

What suggestions above would you be interested in trying if you wanted to feel focused?

...................................................................................................

...................................................................................................

...................................................................................................

It can be hard to focus and remember good things when you are in the midst of a negative feeling. Browse through your 'comfort tool box' on page 91 which will help keep you focused and give you comfort when things get too rough for you.

What have you got in your comfort tool box at this moment?

......................................................................................

......................................................................................

......................................................................................

Alternative coping strategies for when you need to see **blood or pick scabs** include giving yourself an alternative visual stimulus by:

■ Drawing on your wrists with red felt tip pen or red marker pen.
■ Painting yourself with red paint.
■ Painting yourself with food colouring.
■ Tattooing yourself using henna.

What suggestions above would you be interested in using as an alternative visual stimuli prior to you wanting to self harm?

......................................................................................

......................................................................................

Another coping strategy is to 'self talk' by telling yourself to take five minutes before doing anything. Sometimes these extra five minutes will be enough to get you through the moment and may give you a chance to put into practice some of the above alternative strategies which will help you to get through your difficult feelings and for you to stay safe.

What could you say to yourself that would help you with the waiting game?

......................................................................................

......................................................................................

Something you could say to yourself might be 'I will not harm myself for five minutes' and if you are able to manage this, well done, and then try for another five minutes until the feelings pass. You could make yourself a calendar and put stickers on the days you don't self harm and reward yourself when you reach a target set by you.

### DIFFICULTIES IN FINDING SUPPORT

It is very important that you communicate with others about your self harming behaviour as this is the best way to get support from another human being who may be crucial in being able to help you to overcome your self harming behaviour

Who do currently turn to for support concerning your self harming behaviour?

......................................................................................

......................................................................................

......................................................................................

You may feel lonely if it seems to you that nobody understands you or your situation. So when you have the feeling that everything around you seems a waste of time you may self harm to control these feelings of vulnerability and helplessness.

Finding someone who you can trust to discuss your feelings with will bring about the healing process for you. Relationships of any kind are very important to you whether it be with your psychologist, keyworker, doctor, friend, self help organisation or a member of your family who will support you during your difficult times. At times you may have difficulty communicating your need to others, but you must aim to take responsibility and try to find help for yourself.

Make a list of the people you can contact when you are feeling at risk of harming yourself. Be sure that you tell them ahead of time that you may be asking for their support in the future:

. . . . . . . . . . . . . . . . . . . . . . . . . . . . . . . . . . . . . . . . . . . . . . . . . . . . . . . . . . . . . . . . . . . . . . . . . . . . . . . . . . . . . .

. . . . . . . . . . . . . . . . . . . . . . . . . . . . . . . . . . . . . . . . . . . . . . . . . . . . . . . . . . . . . . . . . . . . . . . . . . . . . . . . . . . . . .

. . . . . . . . . . . . . . . . . . . . . . . . . . . . . . . . . . . . . . . . . . . . . . . . . . . . . . . . . . . . . . . . . . . . . . . . . . . . . . . . . . . . . .

There are crisis centres that you can contact, for example, Samaritans, Sane line and others. See list at the end of the workbook. Also, join a self help group. Again contact addresses and telephone numbers at the end of the workbook.

Every year on 1 March there is a self injury awareness day, SIAD, and it is represented by an orange ribbon. Feel supported and support their cause by buying a ribbon and wearing it on this day.

It would be helpful for you to complete a self harming action plan (on page 95) to communicate your needs to someone if you feel overwhelmed by your difficult feelings and also if you need some assistance from them, but are unable to manage this verbally. For example, family, friend, accident and emergency and health professionals. Complete this when you feel well and give it to either family or mental health professionals when you feel like self harming.

Your self harming action plan will bring you closer to having your needs met and understood and by reviewing the plan on a regular basis you can check that it continues to meet your needs or whether you want to make any changes that will maximise your progress.

At times you feel that you still need to use the old harming strategies because self harm is like an addiction and is not an easy habit to break. This does not mean you have failed or gone back to square one. It takes time to change long term habits especially if they feel familiar and safe.

The above suggestions alone are not enough for you to cope with your self harming ideation; these ideas can be helpful if they are working alongside talking therapies; in treatment it is wise to anticipate a series of gains followed by relapses before achieving total abstinence.

Don't give up trying to stop self harming because as already mentioned it takes time to get used to new habits and takes even more time to get rid of old habits. Remember to congratulate yourself on any progress that you make along the way.

## ▶ SELF HARMING ACTION PLAN

Due to experiencing some distressing emotions I am having difficulty expressing my needs to you but I would like some help and support from you.

Please could you contact the following people?

. . . . . . . . . . . . . . . . . . . . . . . . . . . . . . . . . . . . . . . . . . . . . . . . telephone. . . . . . . . . . .

. . . . . . . . . . . . . . . . . . . . . . . . . . . . . . . . . . . . . . . . . . . . . . . . telephone. . . . . . . . . . .

. . . . . . . . . . . . . . . . . . . . . . . . . . . . . . . . . . . . . . . . . . . . . . . . telephone. . . . . . . . . . .

Things you could say to me which would encourage me and help me get through the next few hours are:

. . . . . . . . . . . . . . . . . . . . . . . . . . . . . . . . . . . . . . . . . . . . . . . . . . . . . . . . . . . . . . . . . . . . . .

. . . . . . . . . . . . . . . . . . . . . . . . . . . . . . . . . . . . . . . . . . . . . . . . . . . . . . . . . . . . . . . . . . . . . .

. . . . . . . . . . . . . . . . . . . . . . . . . . . . . . . . . . . . . . . . . . . . . . . . . . . . . . . . . . . . . . . . . . . . . .

Practical things you could do for me which would help me through the next few hours are:

. . . . . . . . . . . . . . . . . . . . . . . . . . . . . . . . . . . . . . . . . . . . . . . . . . . . . . . . . . . . . . . . . . . . . .

. . . . . . . . . . . . . . . . . . . . . . . . . . . . . . . . . . . . . . . . . . . . . . . . . . . . . . . . . . . . . . . . . . . . . .

. . . . . . . . . . . . . . . . . . . . . . . . . . . . . . . . . . . . . . . . . . . . . . . . . . . . . . . . . . . . . . . . . . . . . .

Distraction techniques that I have learnt and need reminding of are:

. . . . . . . . . . . . . . . . . . . . . . . . . . . . . . . . . . . . . . . . . . . . . . . . . . . . . . . . . . . . . . . . . . . . . .

. . . . . . . . . . . . . . . . . . . . . . . . . . . . . . . . . . . . . . . . . . . . . . . . . . . . . . . . . . . . . . . . . . . . . .

. . . . . . . . . . . . . . . . . . . . . . . . . . . . . . . . . . . . . . . . . . . . . . . . . . . . . . . . . . . . . . . . . . . . . .

Any other things I need reminding of that have helped me in the past are:

. . . . . . . . . . . . . . . . . . . . . . . . . . . . . . . . . . . . . . . . . . . . . . . . . . . . . . . . . . . . . . . . . . . . . .

. . . . . . . . . . . . . . . . . . . . . . . . . . . . . . . . . . . . . . . . . . . . . . . . . . . . . . . . . . . . . . . . . . . . . .

It would also be helpful to me if you could:

. . . . . . . . . . . . . . . . . . . . . . . . . . . . . . . . . . . . . . . . . . . . . . . . . . . . . . . . . . . . . . . . . . . . . .

. . . . . . . . . . . . . . . . . . . . . . . . . . . . . . . . . . . . . . . . . . . . . . . . . . . . . . . . . . . . . . . . . . . . . .

It is not helpful to me if:

. . . . . . . . . . . . . . . . . . . . . . . . . . . . . . . . . . . . . . . . . . . . . . . . . . . . . . . . . . . . . . . . . . . . . .

. . . . . . . . . . . . . . . . . . . . . . . . . . . . . . . . . . . . . . . . . . . . . . . . . . . . . . . . . . . . . . . . . . . . . .

| Thank you for your time and understanding |

## ▶ Wheel of 'self harming' end-of-session Questionnaire

What three important things have you learnt and will take away with you from this self harming session (you may need to browse through the session again to jog your memory).

1 ....................................................................................

....................................................................................

....................................................................................

....................................................................................

....................................................................................

....................................................................................

....................................................................................

....................................................................................

....................................................................................

2 ....................................................................................

....................................................................................

....................................................................................

....................................................................................

....................................................................................

....................................................................................

....................................................................................

....................................................................................

....................................................................................

3 ....................................................................................

....................................................................................

....................................................................................

....................................................................................

....................................................................................

....................................................................................

....................................................................................

....................................................................................

....................................................................................

Intense anger and rage is a symptom of your inner distress, but the following session is not meant as a form of treatment but gives ideas of coping strategies to work alongside talking therapies. Hopefully this session will help you to understand why you are the way you are so that you can seek further help through talking therapy.

If you have issues with your anger how differently do you think your life would be if you were able to cope with your anger more effectively?

..........................................................................................

..........................................................................................

..........................................................................................

What would be important to you about this?

..........................................................................................

..........................................................................................

Nothing will happen unless we create a chance for it to come about.

It might be helpful for you to browse through Session 3 again on page 38 to recap on the symptoms of anger.

Below we will be looking at a 'wheel of anger' where each segment represents skills you can learn in relation to how you can deal with these feelings more effectively. Consider each segment, rating each one from 0–10 with 10 being the most difficult skill to manage with regard to your symptoms of anger.

## WHEEL OF ANGER

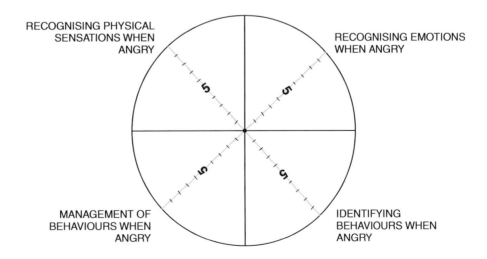

Can you think of the last time that you felt angry and describe it below?

When . . . . . . . . . . . . . . . . . . . . . . . . . . . . . . . . . . . . . . . . . . . . . . . . . . . . . . . . . . . . . . . . . . . . . . . . . . . . . . . . . . . . . . . .

Where . . . . . . . . . . . . . . . . . . . . . . . . . . . . . . . . . . . . . . . . . . . . . . . . . . . . . . . . . . . . . . . . . . . . . . . . . . . . . . . . . . . . .

What happened . . . . . . . . . . . . . . . . . . . . . . . . . . . . . . . . . . . . . . . . . . . . . . . . . . . . . . . . . . . . . . . . . . . . . . . .

. . . . . . . . . . . . . . . . . . . . . . . . . . . . . . . . . . . . . . . . . . . . . . . . . . . . . . . . . . . . . . . . . . . . . . . . . . . . . . . . . . . . . . . . . . . . . . . .

## RECOGNISING PHYSICAL SENSATIONS WHEN ANGRY

How did you know that you were angry; what physical sensations did you experience?

- racing heart and palpitations
- stomach ache
- sweating
- tense muscles – e.g. shoulders, neck, back and head
- feeling faint and dizzy
- shallow breathing – breathlessness, fast breathing
- redness in face
- eyes seem blurred
- dry mouth
- feeling nausea
- shaking
- headache.

List any of the above physical symptoms that you experience:

. . . . . . . . . . . . . . . . . . . . . . . . . . . . . . . . . . . . . . . . . . . . . . . . . . . . . . . . . . . . . . . . . . . . . . . . . . . . . . . . . . . . . . . .

If you can recognise these as warning signs that you are becoming angry this is the first step for you to gain control over your angry emotions.

Once you have noticed your body's indicator that you are becoming angry you need to take notice before your behaviour escalates which might cause you to behave in a way that you might later regret.

You can think of it as a red traffic light – STOP

---

It would be helpful to you to say to yourself:

**When I experience** . . . . . . . . . . . . . . . . . . . . . . . . . . . . . . . . . . . . . . . . . . . . . . . . . . . . . . . . . . . . . . .

. . . . . . . . . . . . . . . . . . . . . . . . . . . . . . . . . . . . . . . . . . . . . . . . . . . . . . . . . . . . . . . . . . . . . . . . . . . . . . . . . . . .

. . . . . . . . . . . . . . . . . . . . . . . . . . . . . . . . . . . . . . . . . . . . . . . . . . . . . . . . . . . . . . . . . . . . . . . . . . . . . . . . . .

'I will stop and think for a moment to where this is going to lead me'.

---

# RECOGNISING EMOTIONS WHEN ANGRY

What emotions did you feel during this difficult time?

. . . . . . . . . . . . . . . . . . . . . . . . . . . . . . . . . . . . . . . . . . . . . . . . . . . . . . . . . . . . . . . . . . . . . . . . . . . . . . . . . . . . .

. . . . . . . . . . . . . . . . . . . . . . . . . . . . . . . . . . . . . . . . . . . . . . . . . . . . . . . . . . . . . . . . . . . . . . . . . . . . . . . . . . . . .

What thoughts were running through your head when you were experiencing the physical symptoms on page 177?

. . . . . . . . . . . . . . . . . . . . . . . . . . . . . . . . . . . . . . . . . . . . . . . . . . . . . . . . . . . . . . . . . . . . . . . . . . . . . . . . . . . . .

. . . . . . . . . . . . . . . . . . . . . . . . . . . . . . . . . . . . . . . . . . . . . . . . . . . . . . . . . . . . . . . . . . . . . . . . . . . . . . . . . . . . .

What thoughts were running through your head while you were angry?

. . . . . . . . . . . . . . . . . . . . . . . . . . . . . . . . . . . . . . . . . . . . . . . . . . . . . . . . . . . . . . . . . . . . . . . . . . . . . . . . . . . . .

. . . . . . . . . . . . . . . . . . . . . . . . . . . . . . . . . . . . . . . . . . . . . . . . . . . . . . . . . . . . . . . . . . . . . . . . . . . . . . . . . . . . .

. . . . . . . . . . . . . . . . . . . . . . . . . . . . . . . . . . . . . . . . . . . . . . . . . . . . . . . . . . . . . . . . . . . . . . . . . . . . . . . . . . . . .

You need to know what you actually are saying to yourself when you are faced with something that makes you angry. Sometimes our self talk is the one that get us all worked up and at times can be based on assumptions or incorrect information. Those who suffer from your disorder often carry a lot of 'baggage' from their past and if old feelings are triggered, they react with feelings as a way of protecting and defending themselves from the hurts and fears of their world.

Anger is an expression of your feelings when you find it hard to communicate to others how you feel inside.

Think about whether your anger is linked towards the other person or is your anger linked to something related to you. For instance did you feel left out or abandoned?

What emotions have you felt whilst angry?

. . . . . . . . . . . . . . . . . . . . . . . . . . . . . . . . . . . . . . . . . . . . . . . . . . . . . . . . . . . . . . . . . . . . . . . . . . . . . . . . . . . . .

. . . . . . . . . . . . . . . . . . . . . . . . . . . . . . . . . . . . . . . . . . . . . . . . . . . . . . . . . . . . . . . . . . . . . . . . . . . . . . . . . . . . .

. . . . . . . . . . . . . . . . . . . . . . . . . . . . . . . . . . . . . . . . . . . . . . . . . . . . . . . . . . . . . . . . . . . . . . . . . . . . . . . . . . . . .

Underneath your anger there is often another emotion, so it is important that you try and name this emotion, for example, guilt, sadness, fear, hurt, humiliation etc so that you can begin to understand yourself.

When angry, as already pointed out, your thinking can get exaggerated and irrational. Try using more helpful self talk and you will find that this will have a more calming effect on the way you feel, for example:

- 'Stay calm and relax'.
- 'Breathe slowly'.
- 'I am not going to let it bother me'.

As already mentioned it is important to recognise that some angry feelings can be left over from your past, especially your childhood, so it is important that you talk over with your therapist about issues that may remain troubling to you.

## IDENTIFYING BEHAVIOURS WHEN ANGRY

What behaviours did you engage in during your anger?

- shouted
- slammed doors
- were verbally abusive
- smashed something
- self harmed
- hit or kicked someone
- threw something
- sulked
- bit someone
- scratched
- others not mentioned.

. . . . . . . . . . . . . . . . . . . . . . . . . . . . . . . . . . . . . . . . . . . . . . . . . . . . . . . . . . . . . . . . . . . . . . . . . . . . . . . .

You must take care and be aware of potentially dangerous situations when you or others may be hurt.

Those who suffer from Borderline Personality Disorder often find that their anger seems to emerge from nowhere and can erupt into a rage; but as soon as it appears the anger has gone.

Has this happened to you sometimes?

. . . . . . . . . . . . . . . . . . . . . . . . . . . . . . . . . . . . . . . . . . . . . . . . . . . . . . . . . . . . . . . . . . . . . . . . . . . . . . . .

. . . . . . . . . . . . . . . . . . . . . . . . . . . . . . . . . . . . . . . . . . . . . . . . . . . . . . . . . . . . . . . . . . . . . . . . . . . . . . . .

Your anger can push a person away, which can be a surprise because that is exactly what you fear the most. But having said that, your anger is one of the ways you communicate your fears. What you need is to find other ways of communicating how you feel to others. Talk to a psychologist who can help you to deal with difficult feelings.

The final stage to understanding your anger is to make a strong commitment to take some action to achieve the goal of managing your anger more effectively.

## MANAGEMENT OF BEHAVIOUR WHEN ANGRY

The next step is to plan tiny steps that would move you closer to what you want.

Below, name the behaviours that you want to change which cause you the most problem.

Behaviours I want to change:

I ...............................................................................

2 ...............................................................................

Below are some positive and constructive ways of dealing with anger:

**Get active**

- run to the shops
- go for a bike ride
- do some gardening
- hoover the house
- bake bread
- go to the gym
- walk around a park
- leave the room to calm down
- clean car
- do some stretches.

**Take it easy**

- play with some clay or Play-Doh™
- do yoga
- listen to calming music
- take deep long breaths
- count to 10
- practice mindfulness
- sing along with the radio
- imagine a peaceful relaxing scene.

**Write it down**

- do some colouring in a book
- write on a piece of paper how mad you are and why and keep writing until you feel some relief. Tear it up and put in bin
- draw a picture of your anger using different coloured felt pens
- write in a journal
- draw or paint a picture.

**Let off steam**

- throw balls
- throw pillows against a wall
- tear up newspapers

- throw stones in a river
- wringing a wet towel.

**Talk about it**

- talk to someone you trust
- ask someone to give you a hug.

**Use self calming statements**

Use self calming statements to 'buy' you more time to calm down and you will be able to look at the situation more clearly:

- 'take a deep breathe'
- 'I must not take it seriously'
- 'I must calm myself down'
- 'STOP'
- 'I feel angry but I must not lose my cool'
- 'I can handle this'
- 'I am OK'
- 'relax and take it easy'
- 'I am getting angry, I need to calm down before I react'
- 'I am getting angry and there are consequences if I get aggressive'
- 'getting aggressive is not going to help me'
- 'Relax my muscles and unclench my fist. Well done I am in control'
- 'It's not worth it'
- 'I will just ignore him/her'
- 'I don't want any trouble'.

Make a list of your calming thoughts and carry them around with you:

. . . . . . . . . . . . . . . . . . . . . . . . . . . . . . . . . . . . . . . . . . . . . . . . . . . . . . . . . . . . . . . . . . . . . . . . . . .

. . . . . . . . . . . . . . . . . . . . . . . . . . . . . . . . . . . . . . . . . . . . . . . . . . . . . . . . . . . . . . . . . . . . . . . . . . .

. . . . . . . . . . . . . . . . . . . . . . . . . . . . . . . . . . . . . . . . . . . . . . . . . . . . . . . . . . . . . . . . . . . . . . . . . . .

. . . . . . . . . . . . . . . . . . . . . . . . . . . . . . . . . . . . . . . . . . . . . . . . . . . . . . . . . . . . . . . . . . . . . . . . . . .

Complete the following new coping strategies using ideas from pages 180 and 181 that you can use when you recognise you are becoming angry:

Instead of doing . . . . . . . . . . . . . . . . . . . . . . . . . . . . . . . . . . . . . . . . . . . . . . . . . . . . . . . . . . . . . . . . .

Next time I am angry I

shall . . . . . . . . . . . . . . . . . . . . . . . . . . . . . . . . . . . . . . . . . . . . . . . . . . . . . . . . . . . . . . . . . . . . . . . .

Instead of doing . . . . . . . . . . . . . . . . . . . . . . . . . . . . . . . . . . . . . . . . . . . . . . . . . . . . . . . . . . . . . . . .

Next time I am angry I shall . . . . . . . . . . . . . . . . . . . . . . . . . . . . . . . . . . . . . . . . . . . . . . . . . . . . . . . .

Complete an anger relapse prevention plan on page 183 and revisit it every three months.

If you still have difficulties with your anger ask your doctor to refer you to an appropriate therapist, mainly CBT (cognitive behavioural therapy) or REBT (rational emotional behavioural therapy).

The above suggestions alone are not enough for you to deal with your angry outburst, but these ideas can be helpful if they are working alongside talking therapies.

Never getting angry is near impossible, but how you act when angry can make your situation better or worse. Don't forget to congratulate yourself on your successes.

> **Don't let your anger control you.**
>
> **Take charge of it!**

## ▶ ANGER RELAPSE PREVENTION PLAN

| **When I experience:** | |
|---|---|
| A *physical sensations* for example: | |
| 1 | 3 |
| 2 | 4 |
| My self calming strategies are: | |
| 1 | 3 |
| 2 | 4 |

| **When I experience:** | |
|---|---|
| *Angry thoughts* for example: | |
| 1 | 3 |
| 2 | 4 |
| My self calming strategies are: | |
| 1 | 3 |
| 2 | 4 |

| **When I experience:** | |
|---|---|
| *Angry emotions* for example: | |
| 1 | 3 |
| 2 | 4 |
| My self calming strategies are: | |
| 1 | 3 |
| 2 | 4 |

| **When I experience:** | |
|---|---|
| *Angry behaviours* for example: | |
| 1 | 3 |
| 2 | 4 |
| My self calming strategies are: | |
| 1 | 3 |
| 2 | 4 |

| **My main motivations for controlling my anger are:** |
|---|
| 1 |
| 2 |

What three important things have you learnt and will take away with you from the anger session (you may need to browse through the session again to jog your memory).

1............................................................................
............................................................................
............................................................................
............................................................................
............................................................................
............................................................................
............................................................................
............................................................................
............................................................................
............................................................................

2............................................................................
............................................................................
............................................................................
............................................................................
............................................................................
............................................................................
............................................................................
............................................................................
............................................................................

3............................................................................
............................................................................
............................................................................
............................................................................
............................................................................
............................................................................
............................................................................
............................................................................

## ► WHEEL OF SELF IDENTITY

Low self esteem and lack of self identity is symptom of your inner distress but the following session is not meant as a form of treatment but only ideas of coping strategies to work alongside talking therapies. Hopefully this session will help you to understand why you are the way you are so that you can seek further help through talking therapy.

If you have difficulties regarding the way you see yourself, how do you think your life would look like if you was able to accept yourself for who you are:

. . . . . . . . . . . . . . . . . . . . . . . . . . . . . . . . . . . . . . . . . . . . . . . . . . . . . . . . . . . . . . . . . . . . . . . . . . . . . . . . . . . . . . .

. . . . . . . . . . . . . . . . . . . . . . . . . . . . . . . . . . . . . . . . . . . . . . . . . . . . . . . . . . . . . . . . . . . . . . . . . . . . . . . . . . . . . . .

What would be important to you about this?

. . . . . . . . . . . . . . . . . . . . . . . . . . . . . . . . . . . . . . . . . . . . . . . . . . . . . . . . . . . . . . . . . . . . . . . . . . . . . . . . . . . . . . .

. . . . . . . . . . . . . . . . . . . . . . . . . . . . . . . . . . . . . . . . . . . . . . . . . . . . . . . . . . . . . . . . . . . . . . . . . . . . . . . . . . . . . . .

Nothing will happen unless we create a chance for it to come about.

It might be helpful for you to browse through Session 3 page 41 to recap on this symptom of self identity.

Below we will be looking at a 'wheel of self identity' where each segment represents skills you can learn in regard to self acceptance. Consider each segment, rating each one from 0−10 with 10 being the most difficult skill to manage.

## WHEEL OF SELF IDENTITY

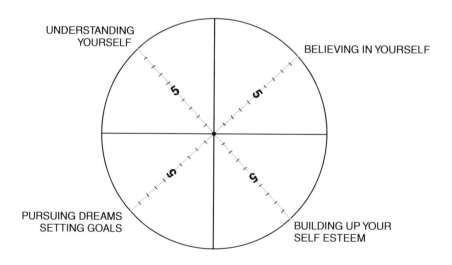

### UNDERSTANDING YOURSELF

When you are a newborn you don't have any idea of whether you are good or bad but as you grow up you learn about who you are which in turn develops your self esteem. You are more likely to feel loved and feel good about yourself if through your early years people have taken good care of you.

While children are growing up, other people, like relatives, teachers, peer groups and others have a bigger role to play when it comes to developing the picture you build of yourself of who you are and how lovable you are. The problem is that if your childhood experience has been negative, for what ever reason, your self esteem would be greatly affected.

To develop a healthy esteem you would have had to mainly experience as a child:

- being praised
- being listened to
- hugs and kisses
- achieving well at school
- being spoken to in a respectful way
- having friends and family that you can trust.

To develop a low self esteem you would have had to mainly experience as a child:

- being bullied
- criticised
- ignored
- teased by peers
- being spoken to in a disrespectful way
- being put down by family and teachers
- experiencing disappointing results regarding your school work
- lack of trust in others
- being treated badly by others.

Has your childhood experience affected your self esteem?

......................................................................................................
......................................................................................................
......................................................................................................
......................................................................................................
......................................................................................................

Some who suffer from Borderline Personality Disorder have needed to protect themselves against the immense pain and hurt that they have experienced whilst growing up. The problem that this causes is that they don't really know who they are because they have buried themselves so deep inside themselves because that is where they feel the safest.

You may need to remind yourself of your identity:

My name is ......................... I am ......................... years old

I live at.................................................................. and my family

consists of ..................................................................

Things I like to enjoy the most are ..............................................

Those suffering from this disorder often feel that whatever their identity is they will never be good enough; this is because they judge themselves too harshly.

## BELIEVING IN YOURSELF

Webster's dictionary defines self esteem as 'a confidence and satisfaction in oneself'.

Do you often find yourself?

- Putting yourself down all the time saying to yourself that you are stupid, fat, too tall, ugly, etc.
- Being afraid of trying something new.
- Depending too much on others to look after you.
- Looking for ways of escaping some uncomfortable feelings.

.................................................................................

.................................................................................

.................................................................................

To build up your self esteem you need to change how you feel emotionally about yourself.

Make a list of all the things you are good at:

.................................................................................

.................................................................................

.................................................................................

Every day you need to ask yourself this question:

What nice thing can I say about myself today?

.................................................................................

.................................................................................

One of the most important things you must do is to say to yourself STOP when you hear negative comments about yourself in your head.

Practice daily self worth affirmations (nice things to say about yourself) which are statements that you say to yourself and after time you will believe them because they are true.

Self affirmations you could say to yourself:

- ▨ I am a good person.
- ▨ I have a good heart.
- ▨ I am a loving person.
- ▨ I am worthy enough to be loved.

Write these self affirmations on a card and carry them around with you so that you can look at them and remind yourself that you are not that bad person when you get a negative comment in your head about yourself.

What self affirmations are you going to write on your card today? Do it now:

......................................................................................

......................................................................................

......................................................................................

You may be saying to yourself that you do not believe the above mentioned affirmations to be true to you personally and that you won't allow yourself to feel worthy of the above statements. The truth is that we are all worthy no matter what we have done or said in the past.

### BUILDING UP YOUR SELF ESTEEM

Think of a character in a film or TV programme who has a low self esteem or does not think much of themselves:

......................................................................................

......................................................................................

What is it about them that makes it obvious to you that they have a low self esteem?

......................................................................................

......................................................................................

......................................................................................

What emotions do you think they are going through which might encourage this character's behaviour?

......................................................................................

......................................................................................

......................................................................................

Does this character handle their emotions in a helpful or harmful way?

......................................................................................

......................................................................................

......................................................................................

If you were a best friend of the above mentioned character what encouraging things could you say to them to help them manage their emotions better?

. . . . . . . . . . . . . . . . . . . . . . . . . . . . . . . . . . . . . . . . . . . . . . . . . . . . . . . . . . . . . . . . . . . . . . . . . . . . . . . . .

. . . . . . . . . . . . . . . . . . . . . . . . . . . . . . . . . . . . . . . . . . . . . . . . . . . . . . . . . . . . . . . . . . . . . . . . . . . . . . . . .

Is there anything else you could do that would help support your above best friend and raise their self esteem?

. . . . . . . . . . . . . . . . . . . . . . . . . . . . . . . . . . . . . . . . . . . . . . . . . . . . . . . . . . . . . . . . . . . . . . . . . . . . . . . . .

. . . . . . . . . . . . . . . . . . . . . . . . . . . . . . . . . . . . . . . . . . . . . . . . . . . . . . . . . . . . . . . . . . . . . . . . . . . . . . . . .

. . . . . . . . . . . . . . . . . . . . . . . . . . . . . . . . . . . . . . . . . . . . . . . . . . . . . . . . . . . . . . . . . . . . . . . . . . . . . . . . .

## HOW COULD YOU BE A BEST FRIEND TO YOURSELF?

- Do things that you enjoy.
- Spend time with people who care about you.
- Avoid those who put you down or treat you badly.
- Self nurture and look after yourself more fairly and kindly.
- Say to yourself positive self affirmations.
- Be brave and take risks.
- Talk to people who can help you let go of past hurts.
- Acknowledge and praise yourself on your achievements.
- Spend more time understanding yourself and express yourself through art therapy and also practise relaxation through reflexology and meditation.
- Treat yourself with love and respect.

We have to learn to be our best friend because we fall too easily into the trap of being our own worst enemy (Thorp, 2005).

How could you start being a best friend to yourself today?

. . . . . . . . . . . . . . . . . . . . . . . . . . . . . . . . . . . . . . . . . . . . . . . . . . . . . . . . . . . . . . . . . . . . . . . . . . . . . . . . .

. . . . . . . . . . . . . . . . . . . . . . . . . . . . . . . . . . . . . . . . . . . . . . . . . . . . . . . . . . . . . . . . . . . . . . . . . . . . . . . . .

. . . . . . . . . . . . . . . . . . . . . . . . . . . . . . . . . . . . . . . . . . . . . . . . . . . . . . . . . . . . . . . . . . . . . . . . . . . . . . . . .

. . . . . . . . . . . . . . . . . . . . . . . . . . . . . . . . . . . . . . . . . . . . . . . . . . . . . . . . . . . . . . . . . . . . . . . . . . . . . . . . .

. . . . . . . . . . . . . . . . . . . . . . . . . . . . . . . . . . . . . . . . . . . . . . . . . . . . . . . . . . . . . . . . . . . . . . . . . . . . . . . . .

On a final note, many of you have suffered more than enough in your life so now it is time that you allowed yourself some kindness because you don't deserve to be hurt anymore. You may have been made to feel bad about things that have happened to you in your life but those experiences are not the real truth about you. You are a worthwhile person who deserves to be respected and cared for.

> **Always remember that.**

## ▶ PURSUING YOUR DREAMS AND GOALS

Look to the future with a sense of adventure and decide on specific hopes and desires that you want included in your life. This might be difficult to contemplate at this moment as your confidence may be low and there may be issues that you need to deal with before you consider any plans for the future.

For now just aim at exploring your dreams and desires and see where it takes you because once you have worked on your self confidence you will then discover your strengths.

Dare to dream and write down the things you would truly desire with regard to:

Work or a career:

.......................................................................................
.......................................................................................
.......................................................................................
.......................................................................................
.......................................................................................

Your health:

.......................................................................................
.......................................................................................
.......................................................................................
.......................................................................................
.......................................................................................

Your relationships:

.......................................................................................
.......................................................................................
.......................................................................................
.......................................................................................
.......................................................................................

Fun and recreation:

......................................................................................................

......................................................................................................

......................................................................................................

......................................................................................................

......................................................................................................

Money and possessions:

......................................................................................................

......................................................................................................

......................................................................................................

......................................................................................................

......................................................................................................

Personal growth:

......................................................................................................

......................................................................................................

......................................................................................................

......................................................................................................

......................................................................................................

Imagine sitting on the veranda in your rocking chair when you are 90 years old, what would you like to be saying to yourself that you have achieved over your lifetime?

......................................................................................................

......................................................................................................

......................................................................................................

......................................................................................................

......................................................................................................

......................................................................................................

Get a large sheet of paper and paint or draw what your true dreams would look like using crayons, paint and pen markers and also stick glitter, feathers, material and cut outs from magazine etc. to make it more fun and exciting.

Write down which day you are planning to do this and add this to your planner on page 139:

......................................................................................................

......................................................................................................

Another way of raising your self esteem is to help others and below are some ideas:

- Sort out your wardrobe and see if you have anything to donate to your local charity shop.
- Give some money to charity.
- Volunteer your time to work in charity shops, Salvation Army or others.
- Ask if your local church might need some volunteers for fetes or morning coffees etc.
- Volunteer to baby-sit for one of your friends.
- Do a good deed for someone.

What ideas do you have whereby you could give someone a helping hand?

........................................................................................

........................................................................................

........................................................................................

........................................................................................

........................................................................................

'Keep walking down the road to who you want to be' and realise that each and every step you take towards healing and knowing more about yourself is you unfolding who you really are (Mahari, 2001).

These suggestions alone are not enough for you to cope with your feelings of identity, but they can be helpful if they are working alongside talking therapies.

## ▶ Wheel of 'self identity' end-of-session Questionnaire

What three important things have you learnt and will take away with you from this 'wheel of self identity' (you may need to browse through the session again to jog your memory).

1...................................................................................................................................

....................................................................................................................................

....................................................................................................................................

....................................................................................................................................

....................................................................................................................................

....................................................................................................................................

....................................................................................................................................

....................................................................................................................................

....................................................................................................................................

....................................................................................................................................

2...................................................................................................................................

....................................................................................................................................

....................................................................................................................................

....................................................................................................................................

....................................................................................................................................

....................................................................................................................................

....................................................................................................................................

....................................................................................................................................

....................................................................................................................................

3...................................................................................................................................

....................................................................................................................................

....................................................................................................................................

....................................................................................................................................

....................................................................................................................................

....................................................................................................................................

....................................................................................................................................

....................................................................................................................................

....................................................................................................................................

We are coming to a close of these sessions now and I hear a sigh of relief, but I hope that the sessions have been helpful for you in understanding your illness. Well done for sticking with it, as there must have been times when it was bound to have been difficult for you, but I hope that your confidence is greater now than when you started the sessions and that you feel a lot more hopeful about your future.

Things to remember are:

- Find out all that you can about your disorder so that you can understand yourself more and the treatments available for you.
- Continue with therapy sessions although you may find them difficult at times.
- Seek support from others who understand you and your disorder.
- Find healthier ways of coping with painful emotions.
- Understand that certain situations may trigger behaviours.
- Stick to your treatment plan.
- Get support in treating any substance abuse.

As already mentioned, what happened to you with regard to your difficult past was not your fault, but it is up to you now to do all that you can to heal your past hurts as there really are people who do understand your suffering and want to help and support you through this journey, so please seek them out.

| Take care. |
| --- |

# Bibliography and Further Reading

## Session 1

American Psychiatric Association (1994) DSM-IV. Diagnostic and statistical manual of mental disorders. 4th edn. Washington, DC, APA.

Beal, C. R. (1993) *Boys and Girls: The Development of Gender Roles*. New York, McGraw-Hill.

BMJ (1997) http://www.bmj.com/cgi/content/full/315/7101/176

Collins Dictionary (2001) Glasgow, HarperCollins.

Coopersmith, S. (1967) *The Antecedents of Self Esteem*. San Francisco, CA, W.H. Freeman and Company.

Harris, J. R. (2006). *No Two Alike: Human Nature and Human Individuality*. W.W. Norton.

Murphy, G. (1947) *Personality: A Bio-Social Approach to Origins and Structure*. New York, Harper and Row.

Pinel, P. (1806) *Mania Without Delirium*. Oxford University Press.

Plomin, R., DeFries, J. C., McClearn, G. E. and McGuffin, P. (2001) *Behavioural Genetics*. (4th edn). New York, Worth Publishers.

Sulloway, F. J. (1997) *Born to Rebel: Birth Orders, Family Dynamics, and Creative Lives*. Vintage Publishers.

Widiger, T. A., Costa, P. T. and McCrae, R. R. (2002) A proposal for Axis II: diagnosing personality disorders using the five-factor model. In: Costa, P. T., McCrae, R. R. and Widiger, T. A. (eds.) *Personality Disorders and the Five Factor Model of Personality*. Washington, American Psychological Association, pp. 431–456.

World Health Organisation (1992) *The ICD-10 Classification of Mental and Behavioural Disorders. Clinical Descriptions and Diagnostic Guidelines*. Geneva, World Health Organisation.

## Session 2

Bedell Smith, S. (2000) *Diana: In Search of Herself: Portrait of a Troubled Princess*. Signet.

Lieb, K., *et al.* (2004) Borderline personality disorder. *Lancet*, **364**(9432): 453–461.

Teicher, M. H., Anderson, S. L., Polcari, A., Anderson, C. M., Navalta, C. P. and Kim, D. M., The neurobiological consequences of early stress and childhood maltreatment, *Neuroscience & Biobehavioural Reviews* **27** (2003) 33–44.

Torgersen, S., Lygren, S., Oien, P. A., *et al.* (2000) A twin study of personality disorders, *Comprehensive Psychiatry* **41** (6): 416–425.

## Session 3

Bailliere's Tindall Nurses Dictionary (1997) 346.

Collins Pocket Dictionary (2001) 443.

Fenichel, O. (1951) On the psychology of boredom. In *Selected Papers of Fenichel*. New York, W.W. Norton.

Lineham, M. M. (1993) *Cognitive Behavioural Treatment for Borderline Personality Disorder*. New York, Guilford Press.

Miller, D. (1994) *Women Who Hurt Themselves: A Book of Hope and Understanding*. New York, Basic Books.

Stern, A. (1938) Psychoanalytical investigations and therapy in the borderline group of neurosis. *Psycho anal Q* (7) 476–489.

## Session 4

*A Dictionary of Psychology* (2001) originally published by Oxford University Press.

Ballou, M. (1995) Art therapy. In M. Ballou (ed.), *Psychological Interventions: A Guide to Strategies* (pp. 68–72). Westport, CT, Praeger Publishers.

Beck, A. T. (1964) Thinking and depression: Theory and therapy. *Archives of General Psychiatry* **10**, 561–571.

Bricker, D. and Young, J. (1993) A client's guide to schema focused cognitive therapy, Cognitive Therapy Centre, New York, 120 East 56th Street, Suite 530, NY 10022.

Foelsch, P. A. and Kernberg, O. F. (1998) Transference-Focused Psychotherapy for Borderline Personality Disorders. *Psychotherapy in Practice* **4**(2), 67–90.

Linehan, M. (2003) Dialectical Behavior Therapy (DBT) for Borderline Personality Disorder. *Journal of the NAMI California*, **8**(1).

Young, J. E. (1994) *Cognitive Therapy for Personality Disorders: A Schema-focussed Approach* (2nd edn.). Sarasota, FL, Professional Resource Press.

## Session 4

Bateson, G. (1972) *Steps to an Ecology of Mind: Collected Essays in Anthropology, Psychiatry, Evolution, and Epistemology.* University of Chicago Press.

Jennings, S. (1992) *Dramatherapy: Theory and Practice* 2. London, Routledge.

Jones, M. (1907–1990 [1982]) *Process of Change. Therapeutic Communities. Series.* Boston, Routledge & Kegan Paul.

Moreno, J. L. (1987) *The Essential Moreno: Writings on Psychodrama, Group Method, and Spontaneity* (J. Fox, ed.). New York, Springer Publishing.

Slade, P. (1995) *Child Play: Its Importance for Human Development.* JKP Publications.

## Session 5

American Psychiatric Association (2001) Practice guidelines for the treatment of patients with borderline personality disorder. *American Journal of Psychiatry* **158**(10): 1–52.

*British National Formulary* 51 BMJ Publishing Group Ltd London and RPS Publishing (March, 2006).

Marieb, E. N. (1989) *Human Anatomy and Physiology.* Redwood City, CA, The Benjamin-Cummings Publishing Company.

Skodol, A. E., Siever, L. J., Livesley, W. J., Gunderson, J. G., Pfohl, B. and Widiger, T. A. (2002) The borderline diagnosis II: biology, genetics, and clinical course. *Biol Psychiatry* **51**: 951–963.

Soloff, P. H. (2000) Psychopharmacology of borderline personality disorder. *Medical Clinics of North America* **23**(1): 169–192.

## Session 6

### Wheel of mood swings

Goleman, D. (1988) *The Meditative Mind.* J.P. Tarcher.

Linehan, M. M. (1993) *Cognitive-Behavioural Treatment of Borderline Personality Disorder.* Guilford Press.

Wilson Schaef, A. (1996) *Meditation for Women Who Do Too Much.* Harper Collins.

### Wheel of psychosis

Ellis, A. (1962) *Reason and Emotion in Psychotherapy.* L. Stuart.

Linehan, M. M. (1993) *Cognitive-Behavioural Treatment of Borderline Personality Disorder.* Guilford Press.

### Wheel of self harming

Berne, E. (1961) *Transactional Analysis in Psychotherapy: A Systematic Individual and Social Psychiatry.* New York, Grove Press.

Favazza, A. R. (1989) Why patients mutilate themselves, *Hospital and Community Psychiatry* **40**(2) 137–145.

Maslow, A. H. (1943) *A Theory of Human Motivation* originally published in *Psychological Review* **50**, 370–396.

National Institute for Clinical Excellence (NICE) (2004) *Self-harm: Short-term Treatment and Management*, www.nice.org.uk

*Nursing Times* (2002) 98(2) 37–39.

### Wheel of relationships

Kernberg, O. (1995) *Love Relations: Normality and Pathology*. Yale University Press, New Haven and London.

### Wheel of abandonment

Anderson, S. (1999) *Black Swan: 12 Lessons of Abandoned Recovery*. Rock Foundation Press, New York.

Bowlby, J. (1973) *Attachment and Loss, Vol. 2: Separation: Anxiety and Anger*. New York, Basic Books.

Mahari, A. J. (16 May, 1999) 'Abandoned Wound'. http://www.borderlinepersonality.ca/borderabandonwound.htm

Maslow, A. H. (1943) *A Theory of Human Motivation*. Originally published in *Psychological Review* 50, 370–396.

Sroufe, A. (1997) *Emotional Development: The Organization of Emotional Life in the Early Years*. Cambridge University Press.

### Wheel of self identity

Thorp, R. (2005) http://www.quotes-famous.com/person/Roderick-Thorp-quotes.html

### Wheel of suicidal ideas

Blauner, S. R. (2002) *How I Stayed Alive When My Brain Was Trying to Kill Me: One Person's Guide to Suicide Prevention*. Morrow.

## Further resources

Albert Ellis site (2007) Official biographical and research site of Albert Ellis http://www.rebt.ws/

ANZAPT (2007) http://www.anzapt.org/index.php?option=com_jd-wiki&Itemid=346

Directory of Chartered Psychologists http://www.bps.org.uk/e-services/find-a-psychologist/directory.cfm

Dissociation World (2007) http://www.dissociation-world.org.uk/dissociation.html

Ellis, A. (2001) Interview with Albert Ellis in *Psychology Today* magazine (Jan/Feb 2001). Document ID 91 http://health.yahoo.com/mentalhealth-treatment/the-prince-of-reason/pt-Psychology_Today_articles_pto-20010101-000035.html

Everything Company (2001) http://everything2.com/index.pl?node=Susanna%20Kaysen

Gabrielle (2007) Self injury a struggle http://self-injury.net/doyousi/famous/

Information on medications http://gsm.about.com/compact/monograph.asp

Information on medicines www.medicines.org.uk

Information on Tranquillisers and Antidepressants (CITA) www.citawithdrawal.org.uk

Mahari, A.J. (1999) http://www.borderlinepersonality.ca/borderhamstercage.htm

Mahari, A.J. (2001) http://www.borderlinepersonality.ca/borderenabling.htm

Mattingly and Melisso (2000) http://archives.cnn.com/2000/HEALTH/08/29/newsstand.ferrari/

Medicines Information Project http://medguides.medicines.org.uk/

Mind (2005) (http://www.mind.org.uk/Information/Booklets/Rights+guide/Mind+Rights+Guide+6.+Community+care+and+aftercare.htm#What_is_supervised_discharge_

(Mind.org.uk 2003) http://www.mind.org.uk/Information/Legal/LegalbriefHR.htm

News BBC (2007) http://news.bbc.co.uk/1/hi/health/7037400.stm

NICE (The National Institute for Health and Clinical Excellence) CG16 Self-harm: Information for the public http://www.nice.org.uk/guidance/index.jsp?action=download&o=29425

(NICE, 2004) http://www.nice.org.uk/guidance/index.jsp?action=byID&o=10946

Saltarelli, J. (2000) http://www.soulselfhelp.on.ca/pboundaries.html

Samaritans (2006) http://www.samaritans.org/pdf/InfoResourcePack2006.pdf

Thich Nhat Hanh http://thinkexist.com/quotation/hope_is_important_because_it_can_make_the_present/8373.html

Warner Company (2007) http://www.crimelibrary.com/notorious_murders/celebrity/marilyn_monroe/6.html

## Useful addresses and telephone numbers

Association of Therapeutic Communities
Tel: 01242 620 077
Web: www.therapeuticcommunities.org

Booklet free of charge DH publications, PO Box 777 London SE 1 6XH
www.doh.gov.uk/mentalhealth 'choose talking treatments'
Borderline UK
Web: www.borderlineuk.co.uk
User-led network of people with a BPD diagnosis in the UK.

Booklet free of charge DH publications, PO Box 777 London SE 1 6XH
www.doh.gov.uk/mentalhealth 'choose talking treatments'

British Association of Art Therapists (BAAT)
Tel: 020 7686 4216
Web: www.baat.org

British Association for Counselling and Psychotherapy (BACP)
BACP House, 35–37 Albert Street, Rugby, Warwickshire CV21 2SG,
Tel: 0870 443 5252
Web: www.bacp.co.uk

British Association of Drama therapists (BADth)
Tel: 020 7731 0160
Web: www.badth.org.uk

Mental Health Foundation
9th Floor, Sea Containers House, 20 Upper Ground, London. SE1 9QB
Tel: 020 7803 1100
Web: www.mentalhealth.org.uk

Mind
15–19 Broadway
London E15 4BQ
Tel: 0845 7660 163
Web: www.mind.org.uk

National Self-harm Network (NHSN)
PO Box 7264, Nottingham NG1 6WJ
Web: www.nshn.co.uk
Survivor-led organisation supporting those who self-harm

Psychiatric Drug helpline which is run by pharmacists

Helpline: 020 7919 2999

Royal College of Psychiatrists
17 Belgrave Square, London SW1X 8 PG. Tel: 020 7235 2351.

Samaritans
Chris PO Box 9090, Sterling FK8 2SA
Tel: 08457 90 90 90
Web: www.samaritans.org
24-hour emergency helpline

Saneline
1st Floor, Cityside House, 40 Adler Street, London. E1 1EE
Tel: 0845 767 8000
Web: www.sane.org.uk

TalktoFrank
Tel: 0800 776 600
Web: www.ndh.org.uk
Free 24-hour national drugs helpline

The Basement Project
PO Box 5, Abergavenny, Wales NP7 5XW
Tel: 01873 856 524
Publications, groups and workshops for people who self-harm

UK Council for Psychotherapy (UKCP)
167–169 Great Portland Street, London, W1W 5 PF
Tel: 020 7436 3002
Web: www.psychotherapy.org.uk

# Index

36774446R00116

Printed in Great Britain
by Amazon